The Skin That We Speak

The Skin That We Speak

Thoughts on Language and Culture in the Classroom

Edited by

LISA DELPIT

and

JOANNE KILGOUR DOWDY

THE NEW PRESS

NEW YORK

Page ix constitutes an extension of this page.

Published in the United States by The New Press, New York, 2002
Distributed by W. W. Norton & Company, Inc., New York

LIBRARY OF CONGRESS CATALOGING-IN-PUBLICATION DATA

The skin that we speak : thoughts on language and culture in the classroom /
edited by Lisa Delpit and Joanne Kilgour Dowdy.

p.   cm.

Includes bibliographical references.

ISBN 1-56584-544-7

1. Native language and education.   2. English language—Study and teaching.
3. English language—Dialects—Social aspects.   4. Multicultural education.
5. Language policy.   I. Delpit, Lisa D.   II. Dowdy, Joanne Kilgour.

LC201.5 .S55   2001

370.117—dc21   2001044113

The New Press was established in 1990 as a not-for-profit alternative to the
large, commercial publishing houses currently dominating the book publishing
industry. The New Press operates in the public interest rather than for private
gain, and is committed to publishing, in innovative ways, works of educational,
cultural, and community value that are often deemed insufficiently profitable.

The New Press, 450 West 41st Street, 6th floor, New York, NY 10036
www.thenewpress.com

Printed in the United States of America

4   6   8   10   9   7   5   3

Design by Lovedog Studio

For Maya
and all of the other beautiful and brilliant children
at Stone Mountain Charter School.

Contents

Part Three: Teacher Knowledge

The Skin That We Speak

Introduction

LISA DELPIT

In a study conducted in 1974 to assess the development of attitudes in preschool children toward "Black English" (BE) and "Standard English" (SE), Marilyn Rosenthal, the researcher, painted two identical cardboard boxes with similarly drawn faces. Two tapes had previously been made by the same bi-dialectal African American speaker, one in African American language (as distinguished by vocabulary, syntax, and pronunciation) and one in American Standard English. A tape player with one of the tapes was put into each box, out of the children's view. Each box was described as a "head" and each relayed the same messages. The voice in each box introduced itself to the children and indicated that it had a present for the child. Later, each box also asked the children if they would give the speaker their crayons. The children were then asked a number of questions, including these: Which "head," Steve [Standard English] or Kenneth [Black English], would you like to get the present from? Whom do you like better? Whom would you like to play with? Whom would you give your crayons to?

Over 70 percent of the time, both African American and European American three- to five-year-olds categorized the BE speaker as African American and the SE speaker as white. Further, most of them wanted the present from the SE speaker because he "had nicer presents." The majority of the children of both ethnicities believed that the BE speaker, Kenneth, "needed" the crayons more, with one European American boy, aged five and a half, saying that he would give his crayons to Kenneth "cause he don't have nothing" and one four-year-old European American girl indicating that she was afraid of Kenneth (Rosenthal, p. 62).

The findings are fascinating. They indicate, according to the researcher, that very young children have developed attitudes toward African American language and assumptions about its speakers that closely parallel adult American views:

> Interestingly, the African American and white children reflected differences in their personal preferences towards the representative speakers of the two language forms, with the white children preferring the SE speaker and the African American children preferring the BE speaker. Futhermore, there were expressions of learned stereotyped images associated with both speakers. Many of these were pejorative toward the BE speaker—identifying him as talking silly, being unintelligible, being harmful, having nothing, and not having drawing ability. . . . The SE speaker was stereotyped as being more gentle, looking better, having better drawing ability, and being the symbol of success (the last idea was expressed by Population B [African American]).*

It should not be surprising that these attitudes carry over into school. In another study done in the 1970s, student teachers were asked to assess eight hypothetical schoolchildren on the scales of intelligence, being a good student, being privileged, enthusiastic, self-confident, and gentle [Giles & Powesland, 1975:3, cited in R. A. Hudson, *Sociolinguistics*, Cambridge University Press, 1980]. The eight hypothetical students were each defined by three types of information: a photograph, a tape-recorded sample of speech, and a sample of school work (consisting of an essay and a drawing). Each piece of information was based on a real child, but the pieces

*Marilyn Rosenthal, "The Magic Boxes: Pre-School Children's Attitudes Toward Black and Standard English" in *The Florida FL Reporter, Special Issue, Issues in the Teaching of Standard English*, ed. Alfred C. Aarons, 1975).

were recombined to give equal numbers of occasions in which each type of information would be judged positively and negatively.

Hudson (1980) describes the study results:

> The question to be answered by this experiment was: what would happen if information from one source gave a favourable impression but that from another source gave an unfavourable one? The very clear answer was that information from the speech sample *always* [emphasis added] took priority over that from the photograph or the school-work: a favourable impression on the speech sample overrode unfavourable impressions from the other sources, and conversely. (p. 208)

As Michael Stubbs contends (in chapter 5), if school considers someone's language inadequate, they'll probably fail.

Our language embraces us long before we are defined by any other medium of identity. In our mother's womb we hear and feel the sounds, the rhythms, the cadences of our "mother tongue." We learn to associate contentment with certain qualities of voice and physical disequilibrium with others. Our home language is as viscerally tied to our beings as existence itself—as the sweet sounds of love accompany our first milk, as our father's pride permeates our bones and flesh when he shows us off to his friends, as a gentle lullaby or soft murmurs signal release into restful sleep. It is no wonder that our first language becomes intimately connected to our identity.

Just as our skin provides us with a means to negotiate our interactions with the world—both in how we perceive our surroundings and in how those around us perceive us—our language plays an equally pivotal role in determining who we are: it is *The Skin That We Speak*.

For better or worse, in our stratified society our appearance can serve to create an expectation of success or failure, of brilliance or stupidity, of power or impotence. Those whose skin color or hair tex-

ture or facial features do not place them within the dominant phe-
notype are often viewed as "lesser than." But our language "skin"
provides an even more precise mechanism for determining status.
The omission of an "s," an unusual inflection, or a nasalized word
ending can indicate to listeners exactly where in the social hierarchy
a speaker should be assigned. Victoria Purcell-Gates sums it up in
the title of her chapter, ". . . As Soon As She Opened Her Mouth!"

The purpose of this 2002 collection is to explore the links between language and identity, between language and political hierarchy, and between language and cultural conflict.

Most of the articles in this collection make reference to African
American language (also called Black English, Ebonics, or African
American Vernacular English), which is, without question, one of
the most vigorously debated linguistic codes in our nation's history.
As early as 1884, J. Harrison attempted to detail in a fifty-seven-
page treatise that the language of "Negroes" was an oddity that
only vaguely resembled language at all.*

This volume also concerns itself primarily with language and
education. This issue of language use in school is particularly vol-
atile. The commencement of formal education is usually one of
the first settings in a person's life when their language may be
judged as right or wrong; when assumptions may be made about
their intelligence, family life, future potential, or moral fiber every
time a sentence is uttered. African American language has had a
particularly stormy relationship with the educational power structure. Schools often see themselves, and are seen by the larger society, as the arbiters of what is proper, correct, and decent. African
American language forms have been considered none of the above.
Thus, there have been continual moves to eliminate its presence
in classrooms, and raging debates whenever it appears that there
might be some move to suggest otherwise.

The most recent flare-up, the so-called "Ebonics Debate," took
the country by storm during 1996 and 1997. The Oakland School
District put forth a proposal that named the language form spoken

---

*Harrison, J., "Negro English," *Anglia*, VII:232–279, 1884.

by many of its African American students "Ebonics." It not only provided a moniker, but the proposal also declared Ebonics a distinct language, not a dialect or substandard form of English. Further, it recommended that teachers be trained in the elements of Ebonics and steeped in aspects of African American culture. Such training, they argued, would enable teachers to create instruction for African American students that would allow them not only to excel in learning standard English, but to excel in all school subjects. This result had already been achieved on a small scale using the program the board advocated, the "Standard English Proficiency Program." Despite the school board's good intentions, the country went on a rampage, with reporter after reporter declaring that Oakland was planning to teach Black slang and ghetto language to its schoolchildren. Several of the essays in this volume refer to the debate, and more details of the battle are described in chapter 3, No Kinda Sense. Also included, as an appendix, is the formal response of the Linguistic Society of America on the Oakland Ebonics debate.

However, this was not the first time African American language and the education establishment engaged in a very awkward, painful, and public dance. After the riots of the 1960s the general public became aware that African American children were failing in schools in large numbers. African American leaders and, later, President Johnson's "War on Poverty" demanded solutions. Educational scholars, casting about for blame, speculated about the cause of the problem and hit upon the idea that the children's inferior language was the cause of their learning problem. With little or no empirical research to back the claims, what amounted to rumors were circulated through articles, essays, and speeches indicating that African American children had a miniscule vocabulary, were nonverbal, had no substantive communicative exchanges with their parents, and were crushed by the noise and confusion in their homes. The Head Start Program, in large part, was initiated to mitigate the "culturally and linguistically deprived" homes of poor African American children.

Linguists, mostly white, began to study the question. The language was mapped and its unique grammatical features, phonology, and semantics were identified. In contrast to the educators, most linguists concluded that there was nothing inherently inferior about the language of African Americans, but that problems might arise when the language of school and the language of home met. Some African American scholars began to take issue with the work of the white linguists, suggesting that, at best, they were unable to really understand Black language because the language did not exist apart from the culture and they had insufficient access to the culture. It was during this period that the term "Ebonics" (black + phonics, i.e., black sounds) was coined by Professor Robert Williams in the early 1970s, when he convened a meeting of African American scholars to study the question from a culturally specific perspective. He proposed that the white linguists were wrong to consider African American language to be a dialect of English, since the linguistic code really had its roots in West African languages. As the controversy continued, accusations of opportunism, self-aggrandizement, and being in league with the government's attempts to keep African Americans disenfranchised eventually led many white linguists to seek other areas of study (Shuy in Farr-Whiteman).

The next major public explosion concerning African American language and the schools was in 1979, when, in what came to be known as "the *King* case," parents from the Green Road Housing Project in Detroit sued the school system for not educating their children, specifically for failing to teach them to read. The judge in the case, Judge Joiner, eventually dismissed all of the plaintiffs' claims except one, forcing the lawsuit to be tried only on 1703(f), which reads in part: "No state shall deny equal educational opportunity to an individual on account of his or her race, color, sex, or national origin, by . . . the failure to overcome language barriers that impede equal participation by its students in its instructional programs."*

*Smitherman, Geneva, "What Go Round Come Round: *King* in Perspective." *Harvard Educational Review* Vol. 51, No 1, February 1981.

The judge eventually ruled in the plaintiffs' favor, and declared that the teachers and the school system had not taken into account the children's language in their instruction, and thus had failed to teach them appropriately. He ruled that the school board had not previously, but now should (1) "help the teachers understand the problem"; (2) "help provide them with knowledge about the children's use of a 'black English' language system"; and (3) "suggest ways and means of using that knowledge in teaching the students to read." The plaintiffs' lawyers did not think the solution, without any accountability or classroom intervention, went far enough. The public, however, went wild. The media once more peppered the airways and newspapers with suggestions that the judge was equating Black slang and improper English with a true language.*

In the Ebonics debate of 1996, in the War on Poverty reports and counter reports of the 1960s and early 1970s, and in the furor surrounding the *King* case in the early 1980s, the public discussions and publicized scholarly research ended rather suddenly, and with no resolution. Still today African American children fail, and still there is much smoke and little light around the linguistic issues that might affect that failure. Two major professional organizations of English educators have been discussing the educational costs of language discrimination for more than twenty-five years, passing *Students' Right to Their Own Language* in 1974 and the *National Language Policy* in 1988. A survey taken in 2000 by the NCTE & CCCC, however, showed that fully one-third of the membership had no knowledge of the positions the organizations had taken.

During each of the peaks of public interest in African American language and education, scholars have pointed out, but with little public attention, that it may not be the children's language that causes educational problems, but the educational bureaucracy's response to the language. These scholars looked more to attitudes held about the language. They posited that the country's perception of African Americans was such that, given the history of racism in the United States, it attached inferiority to all things black.

*Smitherman, p. 48.

Therefore, African American language would be so categorized. In chapter 11, Shuaib Meacham cites James Baldwin as speculating that "within the considerable chaos of American identity, the one predictable constant has been that those things 'Black' or of Black cultural origin, were on the bottom of the social order." Attitudes about African American language appear to develop early and powerfully.

This volume, then, speaks to language attitudes, a topic that the public furor over the years has insufficiently addressed. Further, we attempt to provide teachers insight into the educational dispositions necessary to expand the language repertoires of children, while at the same time maintaining their connection to their mother tongue. Despite both scholarly research and the various public explosions about language and language use, it is clear from Joan Wynne's article (chapter 12), from visits to any classroom, and from the persistent achievement gap between African American and white students, that teachers do not know what to do about language diversity in their classrooms.

While we do present research in this volume to help the reader understand the social repercussions of speaking one or another language in this country, it is not a technical document intended to map the linguistic differences in language forms. Nor does it analyze linguistic codes or speech events via carefully coded transcripts. Rather, it looks to the heart of the matter—the feelings, the beliefs, the frustrations, the dreams—of those who belong and do not belong to a particular language community, and the education of those whose responsibility it is to teach them.

The book is divided into three sections. Beginning with an inward look, the two pieces in the first section tell the stories of more personal struggles with language, identity, and status. The volume's coeditor, Trinidadian-born Joanne Kilgour Dowdy, a literacy scholar and performing artist, explores growing up in Trinidad with the competing forces of British English and Trinidadian. The following chapter is reprinted from the now out-of-print classic volume, *Ebonics: The True Language of Black Folks*, edited by linguist Robert Williams. Here, linguist Ernie Smith steps away from his scholarly role and tells the personal story of how he acquired standard English.

The second section of the book looks at the consequences of language attitudes in the classroom, and suggests means to positively address those consequences. The first two pieces (one by me, and the second by Judith Baker) give real instructional suggestions for acknowledging the language the children speak, and at the same time, helping them to acquire the standard form.

In order to provide an overview of classroom language we have included a reprinted section of Michael Stubbs' *Sociolinguistics*. This piece is an interesting complement to the other chapters because it was written by a British scholar, primarily about schools in England. In chapter 6, psychologist and Africanist scholar Asa Hilliard furthers this discussion by looking at what happens when students who speak a language form not validated in schools (African American language) are assessed by those schools. In chapters 7 and 8, researchers Gloria Ladson-Billings and Victoria Purcell-Gates look at the consequence of speaking a nonvalidated language form in two school settings: the former, African American language, and the latter, Appalachian English.

The final section looks at the language of teachers, and what they need to know about language to become effective in the classroom. Herb Kohl addresses the issue of the language teachers bring to their students, describing the need for teachers to study their own speech in order to assess students' responses to their work.

In chapter 10, the renowned scholar and activist Geneva Smitherman calls out to speech, language, and composition teachers to remind them that the progressive language education policies proposed in the 1970s have still not been implemented. In chapter 11, Shuaib Meacham looks at the preparation of two African American teachers, and at how language attitudes and differences in cultural common sense almost prevent them from actualizing their teaching dreams. And the final chapter describes the path of a white educator, Joan Wynne, as she grows to understand the consequences of this country's language attitudes, not only for language minority students, but also for the students who are members of the majority. She asks teachers to explore unconscious racism in both their attitudes and their practices in order to allow all students to understand the powerful legacy of the civil rights movement, and to embrace it as their own.

PART ONE

Language and Identity

What do you lose when you lose your language? . . . [You pay] the price for it in one way or another—that remaining, fumbling insecurity when you are not quite sure whether you have the metaphor right in the expression that you are going to use and you know the one that comes to mind is not from the language that you are speaking at the moment.

What does the country lose when it loses individuals who are comfortable with themselves, cultures that are authentic to themselves, the capacity to pursue sensitivity and some kind of recognition that one has a purpose in life? What is lost to a country that encourages people to lose their direction in life?

—JOSHUA FISHMAN

CHAPTER 1

Ovuh Dyuh

JOANNE KILGOUR DOWDY

At her mother's insistence, coeditor JOANNE KIL-GOUR DOWDY learned as a child in Trinidad how to perfectly imitate British English, the idiom of the colonizer and of Trinidadian public life. The cost of acquiring this "skill" was alienation from her peers and also from herself; though "the Queen's English" won her a certain kind of social affirmation, it prevented her from relating to friends and stymied the expression of her vital, inner feelings. She bridged this divide later on in life through the creative medium of acting, which allowed her to legitimately occupy many different selves. One's "language of intimacy" must be validated in the public sphere, Dowdy urges, in order to eradicate the schism in colonized societies—and colonized individuals—between master discourse and the language of personal expression.

I want to blame it all on my mother. It is always easy to blame the mother, and more importantly, the dead cannot speak. So from the vantage point of age and the security from retribution, I want to lay down the beginnings of my personal angst over language. When we were growing up in Trinidad, my mother always reminded us that we needed to learn to "curse in white." By this she meant, or I believed that she meant, that we should always be aware that we had to play to a white audience. We could protest, we could show anger, but we had to remember that there was a white way, and that was the right way. I am sure that she had accepted that this would be the case for her children as long as the British imperial sun did not set.

Being middle class and black brought particular burdens and responsibilities. Especially since our great uncle had actually been a past mayor of Port of Spain, the capital of Trinidad. He had met and sat with Queen Elizabeth, Her Majesty, and the Emperor Haile Selassie of Ethiopia. If we were to continue this outstanding tradition of service in public life, whether political or cultural, we needed to have certain baggage. My mother plodded on unrelentingly in her effort to make us deserving vessels of public acceptance. To "curse in white" was the epitome of embracing the creed of colonization. One not only had to look the part, light-skinned, chemical curls for a coiffure, but one had to sound the part, perfect British diction. Maybe it was my actor's temperament that made the language such a personal journey to me. I took on the project of "th"s and "wh"s with such devotion that I was given many opportunities to represent my grade school in choral speaking competitions and story-telling festivals.

Imitation is a grand play when you are young and impressionable. But I can tell you a very painful memory about discovering the edge between fantasy and reality. My friends were out in the middle of the street playing cricket, no less, when I decided to join them. I was never good at sports, my hand and eye coordination is more the product of wishful thinking than reality. But I ventured in, as a good sport, and also as a way to provide entertainment for the group. Again, having the soul of an actor can force you to put your personal image at risk for no good reason except that it gives you a chance to affect the situation to your advantage. Applause drives the reasoning of any self-respecting ham. In other words, anything for attention. So here we are playing cricket, looking out for the cars turning into the street and forcing us to scatter onto the sidewalks, and I hit a ball over the fence nearest my left. It's a miracle that my makeshift bat even made contact with the ball, and that I managed to direct it away from the pitcher. It's another miracle that in the scramble for the fielders to find the ball, I scream out "Over there." Note that the "th" was intact. My English, English teacher would have been proud of me, but more likely, my mother would have been even more excited by my "mastery of the language." The game stopped still for those few seconds while I spoke. Then the giggling and snickering began. Someone was hollering my phrase, "over there," in the most exaggerated British accent. Then the others picked it up. It sounded as strange as any foreign language sounded to me. Who could have said that phrase, was my question? Any sensible person in those given circumstances would have enunciated "Ovuh dyuh!" I was frozen to the asphalt. Should I run, should I stand and stare them down? What was the "right" way to deal with their scornful laughs?

In Trinidad, the sounds of the mother land, Africa, play in and out of the language patterns of Europe, India, and Asia. The Trin-

idadian who has not been made to subjugate her oral history in
imitations of the most recent foreign television star, American or
British, has a plumb line to the African West Coast. The spirits of
her ancestors occupy a chamber in her consciousness that make it
easy to reach back, unself-consciously, to the deeper inspiration of
her linguistic culture.

I, however, was definitely a product of my mother's ambitions.
In order for a Trinidadian to make progress on the ladder of success, she has to embrace the English language. If it means forget-
ting that the language of everyone else around you bears witness
to two hundred years of cross-pollination, then so be it. Your job,
as a survivor of the twenty-odd generations of slaves and inden-
tured workers and overseers, is to be best at the language that was
used to enslave you and your forebears. It is a painful strategy for
survival, but maybe it is just another facet of the kind of tran-
scendence to which the descendants of kidnapped Africans had to
aspire in order to survive the very memory of slavery.

School children are not encouraged to write in Trinidadian. It
is viewed, by our esteemed educators, to be a "dialect" not fitted
to the expression of higher thoughts. Our writers have their books
published by British publication houses. Our best student writing
is designed to be read by foreign audiences, for example the board
of the General Certificate of Education in London. We are supposedly writing so that our fellow Caribbean teachers can read our
thoughts, and English is the best means of communication. Everyone who writes the language, knows that they have to translate
their thoughts as fast as they can speak, if they are going to come
across as more than morons attempting to speak "the Queen's English."

What we've managed to do, as a nation, is to relegate our language to the back room of "other." Our calypso singers, politicians,
and television stars are allowed to speak Trinidadian. But our daily
newspaper is produced in the best English this side of London. I
suppose it is important that Her Majesty can read our daily goings-
on, regardless of the fact that we became an independent Republic
some twelve years ago. So who are we playing to? It seems the

only people who get to question the value judgment that we place on our indigenous language are the cultural workers in the field of poetry and playwriting. When artists represent Trinidadians in their natural speaking state, none of them sound like they are distracted by the sound patterns of the English language.

So here is the situation that my mother finds herself in: she is very light-skinned, she comes from a politically privileged family and she is bright and ambitious. She has children who are light-skinned, they do not necessarily have to use chemicals in their hair to look "good" as in "white-derived," and they obviously have a talent for imitating language. What good mother would not marshal all the available supports to help her children access the power structure that several centuries of black, white, and Chinese inter-marriage delivered to their generation? My mother made every effort to have us learn ballet, take piano lessons, join the choirs that our school formed, and dress in the best representations of British fashion that she could afford. My grandmother was an excellent seamstress, and a co-conspirator in this upward push, so the burden was not entirely on my mother.

Through my mother's and grandmother's tutelage I was on a journey to becoming the "good girl" according to the colonizer's belief system. The more I succeeded in this role, the more I felt segregated from my peers. I used the Queen's English to please my mother and my teachers, and my friends used Trinidadian to express their innermost thoughts and desires. We lived in two different countries, separated by our ambitions for our lives. They were "ovuh dyuh," and I was "over there." I was driven to please, especially after my mother died and I was left with my grand-mother's even more restricted value system. My desire to fit in so that I would have a home to come to after school, or ballet lessons, or a game of cricket in the street, did not figure into the world of my classmates or neighbors. We struggled to achieve different goals for separate reasons and thus, I was left defenseless against the accusations of trying to sound "white."

My brother and sister ran into peer pressure and gave in to it. They never bothered to perfect the tones and diction of the ruling

class. In fact, they spent the better part of their adolescence con-
spiring to pull down every vestige of British domination in their
lives. They joined the national student movement and marched in
the street carrying placards that protested the black government's
involvement in oppressing their people. They painted slogans on
walls criticizing the continuation of British tyranny in the education programs. They were both forced out of high school before
they completed their education. My sister went to secretarial school
and my brother went to work as a counter clerk at the national
airline's main office.

I went to one of the prestige schools that was run by nuns.
Their claim to fame was the level of academic performance that
they managed to cultivate in the all-female population. We were
all expected to be bright, and speak "right." No Trinidadian in the
school rooms. To speak English, one had to practice. We were
given all the latitude in the world to suspend our reality as Trinidadians, the proud survivors of three hundred years of British,
French, and Spanish domination, and to perfect the one language
system that we should have ripped from our throats at the earliest
age possible. Instead, we made our throats moist and forced our
tones up an octave so that our voices matched the quality of the
few expatriates who had survived the independence movement of
the 1950s.

I think that I survived my high school years by assuming the
best mask ever fabricated: the mask of language. I invented a
character who wanted to please her teachers and her dead mother.
I engaged a form of thinking that never appeared to question
authority and also never let slip any knowledge of an alternative
identity. My role was to survive, and to do it with the same finesse
that millions of black people had done over the centuries. Yet I
was determined to beat the system that had been working to eradicate all vestiges of black genius, through its autocratic approach
to education. When I was chosen to be the assistant Head Girl, or
prefect, a low-level representative of the principal's authority, I
created history. I had been officially appointed to the role of "good
girl." But, instead of fulfilling the role as my mother would have

hoped, the Head Girl and I chose to wear our hair natural, so that we resembled Masai women. We brought our Afrocentric identity to the attention of the school, and by so doing, encouraged other students to feel free to express their Trinidadian attitude toward their education. We did not privilege light skins, as was the custom among prefects before us. We were outspoken about our concern for the student population that had previously been ignored or disenfranchised in the school community. Ours was a new kind of leadership, and our fellow students seemed to warm to the challenge of forging a new identity outside of the colonial models that we had been given up to that time. The continental shift from Europe to Africa was evident in our new black pride. We could switch from English to Trinidadian as fast as radar could sound the ocean depths. Ovuh dyuh was now present and center stage for our generation.

By the time I graduated from high school—rather, secondary school, to use our preferred label—I had the privilege of claiming to be a member of a television production company, Banyan Television Workshop. We wrote short skits about local people who were "colorful" because of their use of the Trinidadian language. In other words, you could find these people anywhere we looked. The few people who spoke British English were in positions of authority and they made an effort to impress their power on the people who they were addressing.

This opportunity, to write and act these familiar characters, gave me a new lease on life. The chains fell from around my tongue, and my brain began to feel as if it were oiled and moving along without hiccups. I had been granted the supreme opportunity of an actor's life, my quest for legitimization was answered. Now I could be any number of people from my environment, simply by changing my persona. Even more exciting than that freedom was the fact that I would be shown appreciation for my facility to slip from one mask to the other. I could travel up and down the continental shift, moving from Caribbean to English intonations, without anyone being offended. All the shades of my existence could be called into the performance medium, and I, at last, could feel integrated.

The advent of the television workshop during my high school years meant that I had found the real life flesh to put on the sharp-edged bones of the skeleton that was the English language. Now my soul could find its way throughout my body, and I could feel at one with my inner reality. No more the hesitation of translating Trinidadian to British idiom, no more the self-doubt associated with being perceived as a second-language speaker. But now, at last, I had the dignity of shaping my world as I saw it and the ability to name the world in the way that I experienced it. I now had a choice between the "th"s and the "de"s.

That creative work in the television workshop made my life as an actor very different from my life outside of the theater. In the "real world" I was forced to experience life in two languages: my inner language and the English through which Trinidad's public life was conducted: the news, the foreign television programs, and formal education. The colonizer's language, English, continued to set up a force field against which I had to do battle for my soul. As a result of my acting life, I came to understand and be able to talk about the conflict that I experienced when I had to communicate in the larger world. I now saw that the linguistic tension that I lived every day was the result of a war for the minds of the colonized. I came to understand that the colonizer only valued the native language of the colonized in the realm of entertainment. In so doing, the colonizer weighs the whole issue of the colonized's language, the history and the community experience that it represents, and decides that the value is nil.

The "successful" colonized person understands, with the help of her family's and her community's experience of colonization, that the survival technique for the subjugated group involves double realities. She must be in two places at the same time, ovuh dyuh and here too, and not give any indication that her attention is divided. She must operate from behind the mask of the "white" language. Her lot is to act as a channeler of languages, a mere imitator of the sounds and belief systems, not one who makes sense of the ideas. The Head Girl should never remember the Masai. This is the reality that divides her soul when she attempts to slip from behind her mask of "acceptable" white language and begin to engage a conversation in her own tongue.

There is mental conflict about the priority that should be given to the mother tongue over the master discourse. In the public life, the value given to the patriarch's tongue, the master discourse, always supersedes that given to the matriarch. The "language of intimacy," as Richard Rodriguez calls it, has no place in the public arena. In other words, soul and reality occupy separate linguistic spaces. This conflict duplicates itself in every aspect of life, when the colonized tries to negotiate the two worlds of language by building bridges from one side to the other.

At a loss for words really describes the feeling of the soul in the "white" language world. Thoughts come into her head in her family's intimate vocabulary, and she strains to translate those ideas into the acceptable form expected in public conversation. She expects that her usual facility with language will be available to her when she begins to speak in public. Instead, there are cold, metal sounds bouncing off her teeth, the act of translation cooling the passion of the thought. Where she expected to create an easy access to her listeners' acceptance, she finds that her efforts create a glistening wall, icy with dangerous foreign sounds and echoes of the unfamiliar tones of strangers.

The continual disappointment with the master discourse creates a shroud that covers every utterance with a doubt about its worthiness. The voice in her head does not match the tone in her throat. She sees and hears herself becoming a tape played at the wrong speed. Unless she can reconnect with the sense of familiarity of using language that she grew up taking for granted, she loses all ability to integrate the dominant idiom into her language system and she is rendered voiceless.

So, for the colonized speaker, the issue is not really about whether she has a language or not. The issue is about having enough opportunity to practice that language in "legitimate" communications. The central concern is about having the freedom to go back and forth from the home language to the public language without feeling a sense of inferiority. The issue is about letting colonized people communicate in their many spheres of communication, and not limiting them to jazz, reggae, samba, calypso, and zouk. Let the Head Girl be a good Masai and the cricketer hit the ball beyond the boundary ovuh dyuh.

The war will be won when she who is the marginalized comes to speak more in her own language, and people accept her communication as valid and representative. Her need to communicate, formerly unhappy forays into the unfamiliar territory of alternate language discourse, will blossom into the flowers that had been dormant in the arid land of the desert of master discourse. The status quo that assured her that no one would listen, or that they would complain that her enunciation was incomprehensible, will disappear in an ocean of sound.

In such a time, mothers will no longer have to force their children to act like strangers among their elders. They will hold hands with generations and celebrate the community experience that makes language sensible to all those who are members of the group. Their children will join them in their quest to preserve the ancestral tones and images that represent centuries of love, hope and success. This is when we will all be able to speak "clearly," not just enunciate, and put our soul's reality out in the open.

CHAPTER 2

Ebonics: A Case History

ERNIE SMITH

ERNIE SMITH, now a renowned linguist and powerful public orator, tells the story of his life through the story of his language. From his first experience with school, his language was labeled deficient. School authorities placed him first in remedial courses and then, finally, at a vocational school where he wouldn't need to learn "sophisticated" speech. After graduating, Smith hit the streets. It was out there that he received his most extensive education in language, learning how to seamlessly switch back and forth between Ebonics, the language of the "unlearned Southern Black," and Standard English. Eventually, Smith was inspired to return to school, and he went on to become the speaker he is today. His story is one in which linguistic competence, through all its incarnations, has been the shaping force of his life. Only when "Standard English" was modeled by those whose ideas called for the political liberation of African Americans, did the standard become acceptable to him as a language choice.

I have spoken Ebonics—or, as it has also been referred to, Black English—since I was a child. Because my parents and playmates, the primary teachers of speech and language, spoke Ebonics, it was the language I acquired.

It was not until much later, however, that I discovered there was a drastic difference between the language I had acquired and used extensively in my home environment, and the language I was expected to use away from home, especially in the classroom. In 1948 my family moved to South Central Los Angeles, where I attended a predominantly Black grade school. At this particular elementary school, I was confronted with the fact that my language was different and that this difference was perceived as a "deficiency" that needed to be corrected. There was a gross mis-match between my informal, everyday language style and the formal school talk required by teachers.

Teachers and other school officials often used such terms as "talking flat," "sloven speech," "corrupt speech," "broken English," "verbal cripple," "verbally destitute," "linguistically handicapped," and "linguistically deprived" to describe the language behavior of my Black classmates and me. They suggested that our language differences were deficiencies that were related to physical and/or mental abnormalities. Often during Parent-Teacher Conferences or at Open House Conferences, my teachers were not hesitant to suggest to my parents, and to parents of other children, that we should be assigned to the school speech clinic for speech therapy or to the school psychologist for a diagnostic examination, and treatment for possible congenital mental disorders.

Because I had been labeled a verbal cripple by my teachers in elementary school, my language differences at Junior High were, from the "G-G" (Git Go),[1] the basis for my having been assigned to remediation language classes and special sections of most of my other academic courses. The stigma of having been assigned to the "bonehead" sections of my courses created for me, as well as for other children assigned to those sections, a situation whereby we became the object of mockery and gibes from our other schoolmates. Not infrequently the "signifying" and "hoorahin" of our other agemates would lead to "woofin"[2] sessions or fist fights, which was behavior that teachers and administrators considered totally reprehensible and intolerable. By the time I reached the ninth grade at Edison, I was labeled "anti-social" and described as "acting out." Thus, as had been the case throughout my elementary school years, during my junior high school years, it was always my language competence or behavior that precipitated my negative experiences.

In 1954 I began my first semester at John C. Fremont High School in South Central Los Angeles. At Fremont my language difficulties were again the basis for my assignment to special sections of almost all of my courses; and again the stigma of having been assigned to these remedial courses created situations where those of us who were in these special courses became the brunt of the jokes and teasing gibes of our other schoolmates. Eventually, disruptive language became the grounds for my having been suspended from Fremont High and assigned to an all-boys normal school called Jacob A. Riis.

Jacob A. Riis was a quasi vocational-education, behavior-management institution, where disruptive males who could not adjust to the requisites of a co-educational environment were isolated for rehabilitation or behavior modification. When I was initially admitted to Riis, I was administered a series of vocational aptitude tests which, according to my counselors, indicated that I had a very low comprehension of the English language. As with most children who failed or scored low in English Comprehension on these tests, I was urged by the counselors at Riis to only aspire to fields or occupations that were in the vocational trades or industrial arts. Having been tracked into dull and uninteresting shop courses at Riis, I became totally bored and turned off with school. And although I was verbally encouraged by my teachers because of my "high potential," I was labeled as "incorrigible." After doing a "yard"[3] at Riis, I returned to John C. Fremont and graduated in the Winter Class of 1957. Because most of my encounters with the urban school system were, in the main, very negative, I had no aspirations or intentions whatsoever of pursuing a post-secondary education.

Probably because most of my early adolescent encounters with professionals, Black and White, had been with those I had encountered as authority figures, I developed an intense mistrust and dislike for professionals, especially "boozje"[4] Blacks. Paradoxically, my mistrust of bourgeois Black professionals was due to their annoying language behavior. Because Black professionals were always "talking proper"[5] and seemingly "puttin' on airs," they appeared superficial, insincere, and phoney. Furthermore, because the vast majority of the Black professionals resided in areas out of the Black ghetto, there were few if any professionals in occupations such as doctors, dentists, attorneys, pharmacists, and engineers, etc., with whom I could identify. The absence of role models who were Black professionals, coupled with my negative encounters and reactions to authority figures in general, such as my teachers, truant, juvenile, and probation officers, etc., precipitated a reaction which ultimately was the basis for my belief that formal education was irrelevant, and that I could make it in the streets, "ridin 'n' leanin, stylin 'n' schemin, and talkin out the side of my mouth"; "tryin on clothes, pimpin whoes, and slammin Eldorado does."[6]

In the streets, however, it was again my linguistic competence that became pivotal to my survival. My first street hustle or game was what is called "stuff playin."[7] I was a "slum hustler," i.e., selling inexpensive watches, rings, perfume, and costume jewelry outside of banks and on supermarket parking lots. To become a proficient "con man" or "stuff player," I needed to develop a fluent and proficient use of the speech characteristics and phonology of the unlearned Southern Black. This is often called "jeffin," or "game whoopin."[8] Primarily because most urbanized Blacks as well as Whites associate language usage and speech forms with intelligence, and because they attribute the lowest level of intelligence to speakers and users of the "deep south" variety of Ebonics, this bias or predisposition towards the user of Southern Ebonics made them easy "marks,"[9] for stuff players and game whoopers.

In order to complete a transaction as a slum hustler, there is a strong reliance on two variables: 1) the mark or victim had to have the above-mentioned sociolinguistic bias or ignorance; and 2) he must have some latent drive for "gettin over."[10] Since Ebonics, especially Southern Ebonics, has been prejudicially embedded into the minds of many people as an index of intelligence, most slum hustlers know that by eyerolling, head scratching, grinning, and shuffling, and by skillfully code switching into the language and speech forms that are stereotyped as characteristic of unlearned and illiterate Southern Blacks, they can induce a mark into paying considerably more than their actual value—for relatively inexpensive watches and rings, for example.

While slum hustling is a cunning and manipulative ruse, it does not fall within that category of confidence schemes and swindles that are legally defined as theft, bunco, or fraud, and hence, slum hustling was not a legally precarious hustle. However, because often outraged tricks or "marks" resort to the use of physical violence to get their money back when they have discovered that the merchandise wasn't genuine, slum hustling was indeed precarious in other ways. Needless to say, these kinds of negative encounters created, for me, circumstances which eventually required that I suspend operations and divert my entrepreneurial talents into other fields. In my Aunt Bert's vernacular, I had to "Root hog or die po'."[11]

Sweet Mouthin',
Rappin' and Mackin'

In 1959 I began to diversify my hustling talents into other fields, and ironically, it was again my linguistic competence that was essential to my success and survival. I had, since my early teens, always admired and aspired to become a mellow fellow, player, and a "macaroni,"[12] and while in the neighborhood where I lived there were no professionals to serve as role models, there were numerous bookmakers, gamblers, hustlers, pimps, gangsters, and players.

Walter N., a fellow who I considered to be a top-notch player and a mack, first taught me the pimping game. Schoolboy, which was Walter's monica or nickname[13] in the fast life,[14] taught me all of the psycholinguistics of pimpin' and pandering, as well as the sociolinguistics of survival within and outside the street culture. He especially emphasized the necessity of my developing an ability to linguistically code switch into "proper English." Unlike stuff playin', and slum hustling, which are hustles that required a proficient and skillful use of linguistic, paralinguistic, and semantic cues conveying an ignorant personality, sweetmouthin', rappin', and especially mackin' required a complete reversal in roles. Schoolboy not only taught me the nuances of the fast life, he urged that I pursue a post-secondary education. In fact, at his insistence, in 1959 I enrolled in Los Angeles Metropolitan College of Business.

Because I had scored low in the College English Examination Board Test, I had to enroll in what we called at that time "dumbbell" English courses, and once again I found my success and survival pivoting and hinging on my language behavior and linguistic competence. In 1962, while still a student, I joined the Nation of Islam, commonly known as the Black Muslims. There were a number of factors that motivated my becoming a member of the Nation of Islam: their promulgation of Black pride, Black dignity, Black self-respect, Black self-help, Black self-improvement, and the like, but above all it was the linguistic proficiency and forensic style of the minister of Mosque #27, Brother John Shabazz. I was so overwhelmed by the eloquent oratorical style of Minister Malcolm X of Mosque #7 in New York, that I was convinced that I would not lose any masculinity or Blackness by learning to speak Standard Oral English.

I had originally been taking a junior college transfer course at L.A. Metropolitan because I wanted to become a Muslim Minister. I was encouraged by Minister John to enroll in some public speaking or theater arts, drama, voice and diction, or communication skills classes, which would help build my confidence and develop my own debating and oratorical style. During this period, I became known as a community activist and militant Black Nationalist. I was very much involved in campus and community politics, including the Free Speech Movement, the Civil Rights Movement, Black Power Debates, and the Watts Riots.

In June of 1962 I graduated from L.A. Metropolitan College and received my Associate in Arts Degree. In September of 1962, I transferred to Los Angeles State College and began a double major in Speech and Fine Arts. While enrolled at Cal State Los Angeles, I became a member of the Forensics Squad and embarked on what was to become a quasi-professional career in public address and speech making.

In 1967 I graduated from Cal State and received my Bachelor of Arts Degree. In August of 1967, I began a career in the mass communications media, working at KTTV Television Studios, in Hollywood, as an Associate Producer of a conversation-type talk show, called *The Joe Pyne Show*. I had appeared often on that show prior to 1967 as a guest discussing controversial issues. Trained and seasoned in the nuances of debate and public speaking, and having thus become an associate producer on a TV talk show, language communications and rhetoric played a central role in my life throughout the 1960s, and indeed it was again my language competence, especially my forensic proficiency that was responsible for my success and achievement.

Before 1968, the central influence that language had in my life was occasioned by social conditions and economic circumstances. However, during and after 1968, literacy skills and linguistic competence became one of my conscious concerns. This concern was first aroused by the astonishing number of young high school drop-outs and often high school graduates I was encountering in South Central Los Angeles who were unable to read or write. I began conducting reading classes for the Brothers in the community who wanted so much to learn how to read. Because I had no background in teaching or education, all of the methods, techniques, and de-vices I had used in my attempts to teach reading skills to these brothers failed. This created in me intense feelings of dismay, frus-tration, and failure, feelings that led me into a sequence of dys-social behaviors that I have not to this day been able to completely understand.

I formed a community group called the United Front Against Imperialism. As the Minister of Education of this organization, I was responsible for the creation of relevant reading materials and the development of a valid teaching technique to "educate the masses." The United Front was a Maoist-oriented organization through which I was going to strike a mortal blow to the decadent and oppressive imperialist, capitalist system. I never did.

So I enrolled in the Graduate Program in Comparative Culture in January of 1970. When I enrolled I had not defined any areas of special interest or concentration. I had a little background in drama, speech, and fine arts, and Dr. White, my advisor, was a child-psychologist. Recalling that I had expressed to him a concern with the problem of illiteracy in the ghetto, and the problem of reading in the urban schools, Dr. White suggested that during my first quarter, I should just "rock steady"[15] and enroll in a few courses in linguistics and social sciences. Little did I know then that shortly thereafter again my language and linguistic behavior would provide the basis for what was to become three years of relentless investigation and research for a thesis and doctoral dis-sertation.

In May of 1970, following the public announcement that the United States had extended the Vietnam War into Cambodia, and during the midst of a nation-wide campus strike denouncing the National Guard shooting of campus activists on the Kent State

University Campus in Ohio, I was asked to give an antiwar speech in support of the Irvine Student Strike!

During my speech I occasionally used the parlance and jargon which was for me the most graphic, illustrative, and succinct idiom to describe my feelings regarding capitalism and the imperialistic oppression, repression, depression, suppression, and compression of the Afro, Asian, and Latin American peoples. Needless to say, the students "dug"[16] on the speech and indicated during and after the speech that they felt it was "Right On!" However, two days following the speech, I was indicted by the Orange County district attorney's office and charged with a violation of Section 415.5, California O.C., to wit the willful and unlawful and malicious disturbance of the peace by using what was described in the complaint as "vulgar, profane, and indecent" language within the presence or hearing of women or children, in a loud and boisterous manner. I was, to say the least, astonished at this spurious allegation, for surely I had said nothing in that speech that I considered or had intended to be indecent, vulgar, or profane. The charges against me had been filed by the Campus Chief of Police at the behest of one of the campus's more conservative administrators, Vice-Chancelor L.E., in behalf of two elderly women who were secretaries in his office.

It had always been my view that there was no such thing as a bad word. There were words that annoyed people. In the environment in which I was reared, it wasn't what you said, it was the way you said it that communicated your intent. Thus for me, as I imagine for most Blacks, words in and of themselves have a low priority. For those who speak Ebonics, the context of the situation as well as other cues and patterns of communication, such as intonation, gestures, stress, and pitch are just as important in communicating a given idea as the lexical items. Nevertheless, there I was a verbal cripple, ghetto child of the urban schools who supposedly was "never going to amount to nothing," a Graduate Student in residence in one of the major universities in the Western Hemisphere, and once again my language behavior was perceived as a corrupt and deviant vernacular which needed to be corrected.

Only this time, my language had been labeled as vulgar, indecent, and profane.

Dr. Mary Key

This, then, was the hill that I would fight on. I had always at a gut level regarded the manner in which I spoke and communicated as a valid and legitimate idiom, but because of the repeated negative reinforcement throughout my rearing cycle, and because I didn't have the sufficient technical background of knowledge to refute those who argued otherwise, it was always difficult for me to advance my position without being made to appear foolish.

Dr. Mary Key, who was at the time the acting chairperson of the Program in Linguistics at UCI, gave me the technical skills and methodological approaches that enabled me to steadfastly and confidently approach my investigation and examination into the historical development and the sociolinguistic nuances of Ebonics. I had been informed that Dr. Key was currently involved in some independent research of her own into various aspects, features, and sociolinguistic nuances of Ebonics. Because of Dr. Key's expert knowledge of linguistics and social dialects, especially Ebonics, I beseeched her to testify in my behalf at my free speech Trial. Dr. Key obligingly testified in my behalf: and I am certain that if there is one single factor which ultimately led to my acquittal in that matter, it was the enlightened, and objective testimony of Dr. Mary Key.

I am now working as an educator in the University of California system, where I hope to reach both black students and white students in the educational system and inform them of the problems faced by black people in this country and about the validity of talking about a black experience and a black language in society like ours.

NOTES

1. *"G-G" (Git Go)* is a term which means "from the start or the beginning." SYN: "the jump," or "jump street."

2. *Signifying*: to reproach with scornful or sarcastic language; to jeer, or mock; to taunt with meddlesome, irksome comments, annoying gibes. *Hoorahin*: to drive or provoke a person; goading. *Woofin*: to bluff or threaten in a verbal exchange; verbal combat

3. A *yard* is the term used to designate the amount of time served in confinement or as punishment in juvenile hall, Youth Authority, or jail. (Usually refers to a year, but often nine months, or 3/4 year.)

4. *Boojze—Boojz-wa-zee* (Bourgeoisie). This term is used to refer to the middle- and upper-income Blacks who display character traits of Whites; also used to refer to low-income Blacks who exhibit a very obsequious demeanor.

5. *Talkin proper*: 1) a pretentious use of Anglo speech forms: 2) the ability to mimic with mastery the phonological, grammatical, and semantic cues of Standard English: 3) a hypercorrect attempt to speak Standard English, characterized by excessive malaprops, paragogics, reglariced verbs, R sounds in the middle of words, and the adding of R to words ending in A.

6. The phrase, "Ridin 'n' leanin', stylin 'n' schemin, and talkin out the side of my mouth," refers to the manner in which Black pimps and players drive their automobiles (usually cadillac Eldorados) when they are out in the evenings hustling and socializing. In the parlance of the street culture, the phrase, "tryin on clothes, pimpin whos, and slammin Eldorado does," expresses the ultimate of attainment in their lifestyle.

7. *Stuff playin*: a verbal trick and device; a cunning, manipulative ruse used by con artists and swindlers to deceive a person for monetary gain. Stuff, i.e., worthless merchandise or nothing at all, is given in exchange for money. *Stuff player*: one who plays stuff games. *Slum*: costume jewelry, inexpensive rings, or watches that bear brand names which appear genuine.

8. *Jeffin*: the simultaneous shuffling, head scratching, rolling of one's eyes and grinning (especially in the presence of whites) to put ole massa on. *Game whoopin*: to run a game or swindle someone; to whip (whoop), meaning beat or cheat. Verbal trick or device.

9. *Mark*: an expression used by hustlers when referring to a person who is easily deceived, cheated, outwitted: a victim of a confidence scheme or swindle; the "tricked."

10. *Gettin over*: being successful.

11. *Root hog or die po'*: an expression which suggests that as a hog who is hungry will burrow its nose into the ground seeking roots to feed upon, so must a human who has no gainful employment or means of support apply himself to an equally intense effort for subsistence.

12. *Macaroni*: a mack; a very stylish, neat dresser; an English dandy who affected the mannerisms of foreigners. *Mackin*: pimp; gigolo; playboy.

13. *Monica*: a name associated with a person's personality, often considered a bell of notoriety.

14. *Fast life*: the street culture; the lifestyle of hustlers, gamblers, players, etc., so named because one must be ever on guard, alert, and quick of perception.

15. *Rock steady*: stay on position, on balance; to take it easy, to not come unglued, get emotional or excited; start slowly and then build up steam. SYN: Hang on sloopy. Hang in there.

16. *Dug (dig on)*: To pay attention; to observe very closely; to approve of or delight in something.

PART TWO

Language in the Classroom

NATIONAL SPEECH WEEK, 1917

In 1917, the National Council of Teachers of English prepared the following pledge for school students to recite in observance of National Speech Week:

I love the United States of America. I love my country's flag. I love my country's language. I promise:

1. That I will not dishonor my country's speech by leaving off the last syllable of words.

2. That I will say a good American "yes" and "no" in place of an Indian grunt "un-hum" and "nup-um" or a foreign "ya" or "yeh" and "nope."

3. That I will do my best to improve American speech by avoiding loud rough tones, by enunciating distinctly, and by speaking pleasantly, clearly, and sincerely.

4. That I will learn to articulate correctly as many words as possible during the year.

CHAPTER 3

No Kinda
Sense

LISA DELPIT

When LISA DELPIT's eleven-year-old daughter, Maya, transfers to a school where most of the students are African American, her self-esteem soars. She also transfers from Standard English to African American English. Even while struggling to understand her own emotional response to Maya's newly acquired language form, the author is amazed at how quickly her daughter picks it up. She realizes that her daughter is learning it from friends who welcome her as brilliant and beautiful—"part of the club." She concludes that if schools are to be as successful at teaching Standard English, they must be just as welcoming—of the children, of their lives, and of the worlds that interest them. As an example, she argues that if girls are interested in hair, that is an opportunity for teachers to validate that preoccupation and use it as a many-faceted topic for building academic skills and adding Standard English to their students' language repertoire.

"She be all like, 'What ch'all talkin' 'bout?' like she ain't had no kinda sense."

When I heard these words spoken by my eleven-year-old daughter it seemed as though a hundred conflicting scripts raced through my mind all at the same time.

My mother to her ten-year-old daughter: "Lisa, would you please speak correctly? Don't sound so ignorant!"

Me to a group of teachers a few decades later: "All people have the right to their own language. We cannot constantly correct children and expect them to continue to want to talk like us."

Me, arguing a point with my sister, the English teacher: "Okay, the bottom line is, if you had to choose, which would you rather your children be able to say, 'I be rich' or 'I am poor' "?

My sister's response, with no hesitation: "I am poor!"

I find myself back to the present saying, "Maya, would you please speak to me in a language I can understand!" She responds, grimacing, "Aw, mom!" And, pulling her mouth into a primly taut circle, she goes through what she said to me again, this time enunciating with exaggerated, overly precise diction, "She said, 'What are you people speaking about,' as if she didn't have any sense."

I've carried that interchange, and others like it, around with me daily as I work in schools and other educational settings. What was my response about?

There was at once a horror at the words emanating from my

daughter's mouth, and a sense of immense shame at feeling that horror. What was it about her language that evoked such a strong response?

Maya is a middle-class, African American child whose mother is a university professor. Her first language, her mother tongue, is standard American English. This is the language she learned at home and the language she used in the predominantly White schools she attended until fifth grade. Certainly she was exposed to, and used, casual forms of what has been referred to as Black English or Ebonics, which is typical in "M-m-m g-i-r-r-r-l, that sweet potato pie is smokin'! I don't know how you do it, but that pie is callin' my name!"

When Maya was in the middle of the fifth grade, I became concerned with her emotional state in a small, predominantly White private school. Although the instruction was excellent, she seemed to be sinking into some sort of emotional abyss. Although her class had several African American boys, she was the only African American girl. She was often excluded by the other girls. She began to say things like, "Maybe if I were prettier I'd have more friends." When she approached me one day and requested that she be allowed to get plastic surgery because her lips were "too big," I knew I had to act. She transferred midyear to a new start-up public charter school with a population of about 98 percent African American children.

As she developed new friends, her self-esteem soared and once more she became the funny, creative, self-assured kid I recognized. But she also acquired new speech codes. And while my head looked on in awe at how my child could so magically acquire a second language form, at how brilliant her mind was to be able to adapt so readily to new circumstances, my heart lurched at some unexamined fear because she had done so.

As I sought to examine my reaction, I realized there were two questions lurking in my consciousness. The first, why did I react with such heart-pounding emotion to my daughter's words? The second, if it was that easy for my child to "pick up" at school a new language clearly not her home language, then what was pre-

venting the millions of African American children whose home
language was different from the school's from acquiring the dialect
of Standard English? In attempting to answer the first, I gained
insight into the second.

Initially, I wondered if I had been infected by that collective
shame we African Americans have internalized about our very beings. Having come of age in a racist society, we double-think every
aspect of our beings—are we good enough to be accepted by the
white world? If it feels right, then it must be wrong. We have to
change our natural selves to just be adequate. I used to think that
our biggest communal shame was our hair. We have spent millions
of hours and tens of millions of dollars to acquire the "swing hair"
that white American society says is beautiful. I remember when I
returned home from my first year of college with an Afro and
discovered that my mother, who remained publicly stalwart
through most of the tragedies of her life, was overcome by tears
in restaurants, gas stations, and drug stores over what her daughter
"had done to herself." From discussions with friends, that story is
in no way unique in our collective history. When the Oakland
School Board gave birth to the "Ebonics debate" in 1996, I realized
that language might be an even greater source of collective dis-
grace.

Although the purpose of the now infamous Oakland Policy was
to allow teachers to gain enough knowledge about the home language of children to respect it and learn to use it to build knowledge of "standard English," African Americans in all walks of life
were incensed. How dare anyone suggest that that ignorant-
sounding trash was "our language," that we couldn't learn to speak
properly? Do they think we're all stupid? From Kweisi Mfume,
head of the NAACP, to Rev. Jesse Jackson to Maya Angelou, all
expressed to sensation-crazed reporters—with no knowledge of the
real policy—that what Oakland was doing was a terrible, grievous
mistake. Maya Angelou spoke with quiet intensity, "I am incensed.
The very idea that African American language is a language separate and apart can be very threatening because it can encourage
young men and women not to learn standard English." Jesse Jack-

son fired out with his customary passionate oratory, "You don't have to go to school to learn to talk garbage."*

As the media created a mounting furor, never were African American linguistic experts consulted. For that matter, neither were the teachers who were implementing the program. Aileen Moffitt, a white teacher trained in the Standard English Proficiency Program (on which the Oakland policy was based), posted an open letter on the Internet in 1997 [members.tripod.com] in which she praised the effect of the program on her students' achievement and on her own teaching. Never was this kind of information brought to the general public. The black radio stations had a field day. One parodied the televised advertisements for a mail order reading program by presenting fictional endorsements by several characters, including a white cab driver, "Hooked on Ebonics worked for me! Since I got dat stuff, I ain't had nobody stealin' mah money no more!" And another from a professional basketball player: "Hooked on Ebonics worked for me! Ah plays basketball and ah makes millions of dollars. If you gets Hooked on Ebonics, you can be a millionaire, too, jes' like me!" One group, "Atlanta's Black Professionals," managed to get a full-page ad in the *New York Times* (October 9, 1998), without paying a penny. The ad depicts a black man in an overcoat with his back facing the reader, but clearly intended to resemble Dr. Martin Luther King. The headline, "I HAS A DREAM" is written over the image. Below the picture are two paragraphs of small print, with the words, "SPEAK OUT AGAINST EBONICS" printed in large type at the end. In apparent support of the message portrayed by the ad, the Newspaper Association of America awarded it the prestigious Annual Athena Award for 1998 (www.naa.org/display/athena98/grandprize.html).†

---

*Year in Review, 1996, cnn.com.

†I was included in a group of linguists and scholars from all over the country who attempted unsuccessfully to get the *New York Times* to offer equal space for a rebuttal of the ad. The editors refused to publish either the ad or a letter to the editor.

Behind the humor and outrage was the shame that some group of black folks had dared to air our dirty little secret—that a lot of us didn't know how to "talk right," and some didn't much care what other folk thought about it. The even deeper secret was that even those of us who had acquired the "standard dialect" still loved and used aspects of Ebonics all the time. From the call and response rhyming speeches of Reverend Jackson, to the perfectly rendered voices of Alice Walker's, Toni Morrison's, and Zora Neale Hurston's heart-touching characters, to the jivin' d.j.'s on all the Black radio stations, to all of our mothers, brothers, and ourselves, our language has always been a part of our very souls. When we are with our own, we revel in the rhythms and cadences of connection, in the "sho nuf"s, and "what go roun' come roun' "s, and in the "ain' nothin' like the real thing' "s. So what was the problem?

The real issue was our concern about what others would think. We worried how, after years and years of trying to prove ourselves good enough, we might again be dismissed as ignorant and un-worthy by those in power, by "the white folks." We worried that our children would be viewed, and subsequently treated, as "less than"—in schools now, and in the workplace later. Consequently, those of us who reach for or attempt to maintain middle-class acceptability work hard to stamp out the public expression of the language with which we enjoy such a love/hate relationship.

Our fears are not unfounded. When I searched the Internet during the Ebonics debate, I found some of the most horrendous racist comments I could have imagined. Although I cannot find the exact quote, I believe I paraphrase pretty accurately what one man wrote: "Well, the niggers have finally admitted what we all knew all along. They are just too stupid to learn to speak English like the rest of us." Other comments echoed the same sentiments—if in slightly more polite words—that the language spoken by many African Americans was merely further evidence of their cog-nitive deficiency.

Recently, a friend who is a speech pathologist told me about one of her current clients. A major national consulting firm con-tacted my friend and asked if she could work with one of their employees on language improvement. Apparently, the employee was absolutely brilliant in computer technology, but problems arose each time she was sent out on a job. The hiring company invariably called the consulting firm and requested they send someone more knowledgeable. Even after the consulting firm assured the company representatives that this woman was absolutely the best in the country for what they wanted, they still balked. The consultant in question is an African American woman whose speech patterns reflect her Southern, rural roots. None of the companies that hired her could move past her language to appreciate her expertise. Indeed, just before the consulting firm contacted the speech pathologist, one company had sent the firm a long, insulting letter listing every word the consultant had "mispronounced" and every grammatical "mistake" she had made. The consulting firm desperately wanted her expertise, but needed it to be packaged in a form that was acceptable to its clients. Perhaps we have in our country's development reached a stage in which some of the American populace is willing to see beyond skin color to access intellectual competence, but there are as yet few pockets which can "listen beyond" language form.

So, when my child's language reflects that of some of her peers, I feel the eyes of "the other" negatively assessing her intelligence, her competence, her potential, and yes, even her moral fiber. So, I forgive myself for my perhaps overly emotional reaction, my painful ambivalence, for I know that it is less a rejection of the language form created by my people, and more a mother's protective instinct to insure that her child's camouflage is in order when she must encounter potential enemy forces.

But my child has other thoughts on the matter. I ask her if she knows why I critique her language, if she understands that there will be people who judge her on the basis of the words that she speaks. She answers, without hesitation, "Well, that's their problem!" And I hear my own words spoken back to me: "It doesn't matter what other people think about you, you have to be who you are. It's their problem if they can't appreciate how wonderful you are." I try another tack. "You're right, it is their problem. But suppose they are in charge of whether you get the job you want or the college you want to attend?" "Mom," she grins back at me, "you don't have to worry about me." "And just why is that?" She answers with a cheery nonchalance, " 'Cause I know how to code switch!" "Code switch," I repeat in astonishment. "Where did you hear that term?" The eleven year-old who has accompanied me to conferences and speaking engagements since she was an infant answered, "You know, I do listen to you sometimes!" as she bolts out of the door to ride her new scooter.

This code-switching business pushes my thinking. She is, of course, absolutely right. She and many of her friends do know how to code switch. Indeed, after further questioning, I learn that they even have names for the various codes they easily switch to and from, two of my favorites being "ghetto" and "chetto" (pronounced "ketto"). The first is probably self-explanatory, the second, they tell me—being Southern children, after all—is "a combination of 'country' and 'ghetto'."

This metalinguistic facility is amazing, and brings me to my second question. How is it that we spend upwards of twelve years trying to get the standard English dialect into the heads of African American children, when my daughter, and many more like her (including some middle-class White children who go to school with African American children) acquire additional dialects almost as quickly and easily as they change sneaker brand allegiances. Clearly it is not due to a high number of "contact hours" with the new dialect. The only contact is really in school and most of school time is devoted to listening to teachers talk. No, there must be another explanation. I have come to realize that acquiring an additional code comes from identifying with the people who speak it, from connecting the language form with all that is self-affirming and esteem-building, inviting and fun. When we're relaxed and enjoying ourselves on a long-awaited vacation, many of us tend to take on aspects of the lilt of the Irish or the rhythm of Caribbean speech patterns. We do it subconsciously because we associate the language with good times.

Through his study of second-language acquisition, Stephen

Krashen distinguishes the processes of conscious learning (rule-based instruction) from unconscious acquisition ("picking up" a language in a social setting). Krashen found unconscious acquisition to be much more effective. In further studies, however, he found that in some cases people did not easily acquire the new language form. This led him to suggest what he called an affective filter. The filter operates "when affective conditions are not optimal, when the student is not motivated, does not identify with the speakers of the second language, or is overanxious about his performance,... [creating] a mental block ... [which] will prevent the input from reaching those parts of the brain responsible for language acquisition."* In other words, the less stress and the more fun connected to the process, the more easily it is accomplished. When she left her previous school, Maya's self-esteem was low. She considered herself an outcast, once even referring to herself as among the "dregs" of the school. When she arrived at her new school, she was embraced by the children there. She was invited into the group, appreciated for what she brought, and she found that her interests were a vital part of these children's culture. In Krashen's words, her affective filter was lowered and she subconsciously embraced the language of her new friends, as she felt embraced by them.

How does this differ from schools' attempts to produce standard English speakers? First of all, students rarely get to talk in classrooms. The percentage of talk by the teacher far outweighs that by all the students put together. When students do get a chance to speak, if anyone uses what the teacher considers to be "bad English," the transgressor is told that he or she is speaking incorrectly and must "fix" the language in order to gain a response: "Say it right or don't say it at all," or an even harsher equivalent. Secondly, the standard dialect is embedded in instruction that has little connection to children's cultural lives and personal interests. Children are taught through worksheets or textbooks that make no

*Stephen D. Krashen, *Principles and Practices in Second Language Acquisition* (New York: Pergamon, 1982).

reference to their lived experiences. Teachers seldom know much about the children's lives and communities outside of the classroom and either don't know how to or aren't willing to connect instruction to issues that matter to students, their families, and their community. Nowhere is the student's very personhood acknowledged or celebrated. Thirdly, the children whose language is considered defective are themselves viewed as defective. Spoken language has been shown to be one of the key means that teachers, like the corporate world, use to assess the intellect of individuals (Ray Rist). There are doubts in the school adults' minds about some children's cognitive competence since they don't "sound" intelligent.

Finally, there is little in the curriculum that apprises the students of their intellectual legacy—of the fact that people who look like them created much of the knowledge base of today's world. When instruction is stripped of children's cultural legacies, then they are forced to believe that the world and all the good things in it were created by others. This leaves students further alienated from the school and its instructional goals, and more likely to view themselves as inadequate. In short, it would appear that every feature of Krashen's affective filter is in place in the school's attempt to "teach" the standard dialect. The students don't identify with the teachers who question their intelligence or with a curriculum that ignores their existence. They have little opportunity to speak, and become overanxious about being corrected when they do. Subsequently, even when given teacher-sanctioned speaking opportunities, they opt not to. And they are not motivated to learn the new dialect because nothing presented within it connects to their own interests.

I, however, don't believe this need be the case. Watching Maya and her friends skillfully and easily acquire a second code, I am compelled to look for ways that their accomplishment might be replicated in a classroom context. One of the first measures that must be addressed is connected to the Ebonics debate and the Oakland policy which precipitated it. The Oakland School Board realized that as long as teachers viewed children who spoke a particular language form as deficient, then no amount of instructional modification would make much difference. Therefore, they sought to help teachers understand that no language form was better than another from a linguistic or cognitive standpoint. Further, they wanted teachers to understand that Ebonics was rule-based, just like the standard dialect, and that those rules had an historic basis in West African languages. Once teachers really internalize these facts, then it is much more difficult for them to judge their students' abilities solely on the basis of their language form. If the students feel the linguistic equivalent of Maya's feeling the need to be prettier in order to have friends, or having to have lip reduction plastic surgery in order to be acceptable, then they will eventually reject those who make them feel inferior and unacceptable. Just as Maya's new friends made her feel beautiful, brilliant, and "part of the club," teachers have to create similar conditions for their students. If students are to acquire a second language form in school, teachers must not only see their students as nondeficient, they must understand their brilliance, and the brilliance of their home language. To quote Aileen Moffitt, the White teacher in Oakland who published the open letter on the Internet during the Ebonics mania: "[As a result of studying Ebonics through the Oakland Standard English Proficiency Project] I have also developed an appreciation of the language. Ebonics has a richness that goes beyond the obvious features (of grammar, syntax, phonology, phonetics, morphology, and semantics). There are also characteristics of the non-verbal, the gestural, the rhythmic, and the emotional quality of the speech. I may be fluent in the grammatical rules of Ebonics, but I am definitely NOT proficient in these other qualities. Yet I can appreciate and admire them for the richness of expression that they provide. Poetry in Ebonics (including Maya Angelou's) can be music to my ears".*

Secondly, if we are to invite children into the language of school, we must make school inviting to them. In almost every school I have visited, private conversations with children will elicit the

*January 26, 1997, http://members.tripod.com~cdorsett/aileen.htm.

same response: Almost no one in the school ever listens to them. There is no more certain a way to insure that people do not listen to you as to not listen to them. Furthermore, by not listening, teachers cannot know what students are concerned about, what interests them, or what is happening in their lives. Without that knowledge it is difficult to connect the curriculum to anything students find meaningful. And just how do we do that, even if we want to connect children's lives to the curriculum? After all, isn't school about what kids need to know, not what interests them? There are many possible examples, but I will proffer only a few.

I have spent a great deal of time in schools, most recently in one middle school that is 98 percent African American. I was often at the school during its weekly assembly, and at every assembly the teachers spent a good chunk of time berating the students for engaging in grooming during school or class time. "You don't comb your hair at school. You comb it in the morning and you leave it alone. You are not here for a beauty pageant, you are here to learn." Etc., etc., etc. I knew the kids were pretty much ignoring the lectures because even I was tired of hearing it. Furthermore, I had seen little or no change in their behavior—the hair combing continued. Of course anyone who has been anywhere near a middle school knows that there are few things of more interest to eighth-grade girls (and nowadays boys) than hair. Indeed, many African American girls will tell you that they want to be hairdressers. Although it had not apparently dawned on the teachers, it was clear that nothing they said was going to change the students' behavior. I had been thinking about all this for a few days when I woke up in the middle of one night with the thought, "Okay, if those kids want to do hair, we're going to do hair!"

A staple in most twelve-year-old African American girls' bookbag is a bottle of "Luster's Pink Oil Lotion Moisturizer." The first step was to give a bottle of this to the science teacher. His job was to develop a unit on the chemical content of the hair dressing (and other popular hair and makeup products). Students could learn the names and properties of the chemicals and what other purposes they served. They would also learn the effects of these chemicals on human beings. The teacher could further have students explore the processes for testing the products by contacting the pertinent companies. Next was a trip to the Internet, where I found the work of Dr. Gloria Gilmer. Dr. Gilmer is an ethnomathematician (one who looks at mathematics through a cultural lens), and founding President of the International Study Group on Ethnomathematics.* Dr. Gilmer created a unit on patterns and tesselations (filling up a two-dimensional space by congruent copies of a figure that do not overlap) by studying African braiding. She interviewed braiders, along with students and teachers, and then developed several classroom activities as a result of the interviews, including 1) Draw a tesselation using an octagon and square connected along a side as a fundamental shape, and 2) Have a hairstyle show featuring different tesselations. As I read Dr. Gilmer's ideas, I thought of other ideas that would use braiding as a basis for academic studies:

Have students interview braiders as to the cultural significance of the patterns.

Study symmetry and asymmetry in corn rows.

Since most braiders are from Africa, interview the braiders as to what is going on in their home countries and why they decided to leave.

Create a linguistic map of Africa based on the interviews.

I also found a Web site that traced hairstyles through history (www.queensnewyork.com/history/hair.html) and found wonderful tidbits about a subject that has apparently interested humankind since the dawn of history. For instance, Sumerian noblewomen dressed their hair in a heavy, netted chignon, rolls and plaits, powdered it with gold dust or scented yellow starch, and adorned it with gold hairpins and other ornaments; Babylonian and Assyrian men dyed their long hair and square beards black, and crimped and curled them with curling irons; and in classical Greece the

*www.math.buffalo.edu/mad/special/gilmer-gloria__HAIRSTYLES.html.

upper classes used curling irons, and some women dyed their hair red (or in Athens, even blue, dusted with gold, white, or red powder). The site referred to the hairstyles of many other cultures and time periods, and could provide the perfect entrée into the study of history for the girls in question.

Since so many of these girls say that they want to be hairdressers when they grow up, I decided to look into what is entailed in being a successful cosmetologist. I found that it was ideal to have a working knowledge of bookkeeping/record keeping; marketing; small business operation and entrepreneurship; chemistry; anatomy; physiology; basic psychology; public speaking; interpersonal communication; and computer operations. Furthermore, they would have to use math to formulate chemicals for different hair types; study angles so as to achieve the right amount of layers or volume; study biology, anatomy, and chemistry to obtain the knowledge to give proper facial treatments for a particular skin type or structure and to maintain proper hygiene. Finally, in order to use the various kinds of electrical apparatus needed in their trade, cosmetologists need to understand galvanic and faradic currents.

With some attention and thought, any teacher should be able to create a curriculum for many school-based subjects from that spectrum of topics. The object is not to lower standards or just teach what is interesting to the students, but to find the students' interests and build an academic program around them. Learning a new language form is not just a matter of teaching language. It is teaching, period. How we do it affects how children choose to talk. When students' interests are addressed in school, they are more likely to connect with the school, with the teacher, with the academic knowledge, and with the school's language form. Just as Maya found her interests reflected by her new schoolmates and subsequently adopted their language form, so students who find their interests reflected in their school would likely do the same.

The final aspect of my thinking on how schools can change their modus operandi to better enable students to reduce their affective filter and gain access to the standard dialect also stems from Maya's example. Just as she felt inadequate—"less than," one of the "dregs"—before leaving her former school, so many African American children feel upon entering any school. We have not fully realized the extent to which the media and general American belief systems have permeated the consciousness of African American children. Many have internalized the beliefs of the larger society that they and people who look like them are less than the intellectual norm. From media portrayals of African American criminals, to news broadcasts which ignore the positive models of African American maleness, to a focus in schools on slavery rather than on the brilliance of the African intellectual legacy, children come to believe that there is nothing in their heritage to connect to schooling and academic success.

Recently, a young student teacher confessed to me that she did not know what to say when an African American middle-school boy said to her, "So, Ms. Summers, they made us the slaves because we're dumb, huh?" I have spoken often of the young teenager who wondered why I was trying to teach her multiplication because "Black people don't multiply, they just add and subtract. White people multiply!" And then there was the young man whose teacher asked him to look in a mirror and tell her what he saw. His response, "I don't see nothin'." Those of us who teach must first make our students recognize their potential brilliance. When we know the real history of Africa—the Egyptian wonders of technology and mathematics, the astronomical genius of the Mali Dogon, the libraries of Timbuktu—then we can teach our children that if they do not feel they are brilliant, then it is only because they do not know whence they came. Their not achieving is not the way things should be, but a serious break in the history of the world.

What happens when we do so, when we convince them that they come from brilliance, when we encourage them to understand their amazing potential? When they recognize that we believe in them, then they come to trust us, to accept us, to identify with us, and to emulate us. They will come, as Maya came, to adopt aspects of who we are, including our language. If we were to put all of these classroom techniques to work, we would create schools in which children would more readily learn the standard dialect. Moreover, we would create settings in which children would learn all that we wish to teach them. Language form, after all, is merely one small part of a desired curriculum.

So, how do my two initial questions intersect? What is the connection between my emotional response to Maya's new-found language and the fact that schools fare so dismally in teaching the standard dialect? I propose that the negative responses to the children's home language on the part of the adults around them insures that they will reject the school's language and everything else the school has to offer. What can it mean to a child who encounters an adult whose goal is to "Speak Out Against Ebonics"? It can only represent the desire to speak out against those who are speakers of Ebonics—to stamp out not only the child, but those from whom the child first received nurturance, from whom she first felt love, for whom she first smiled. There is a reason our first language is called our mother tongue. To speak out against the language that children bring to school means that we are speaking out against their mothers, that their mothers are not good enough to be a part of the school world. And in the African American community, talking about someone's mother is the worst form of insult!

Ironically, the more determined we are to rid the school of children's home language, the more determined they must become to preserve it. Since language is one of the most intimate expressions of identity, indeed, "the skin that we speak," then to reject a person's language can only feel as if we are rejecting him. But what if we really do want what is good for the African American children in our care? What if we only want to protect them from the deprecating opinions of the larger society? What if we only want to provide them with the tools needed for success in the mainstream? Despite any good intentions, if we cannot understand and even celebrate the wonders of the language these children bring with them to the school—the language forged on African soil, tempered by two hundred years of love, laughter, and survival in the harshest of conditions—then we have little hope of convincing them that we hold their best interests at heart. If we are truly to add another language form to the repertoire of African American children, we must embrace the children, their interests, their mothers, and their language. We must treat all with love, care, and respect. We must make them feel welcomed and invited by allowing their interests, culture, and history into the classroom. We must reconnect them to their own brilliance and gain their trust so that they will learn from us. We must respect them, so that they feel connected to us. Then, and only then, might they be willing to adopt our language form as one to be added to their own.

CHAPTER 4

Trilingualism

JUDITH BAKER

JUDITH BAKER is a high school English teacher who has discovered that when students know that their "home" language is respected, they can be fascinated by a study of the different "Englishes" they speak. They hear the southern roots in the language of an African American student who has lived his entire life in Boston and see how the grammar of Spanish (or Vietnamese or Russian or Haitian) makes patterns in the way in which first- or even second-generation immigrant students speak. When formal English no longer threatens to demean them, students are more than willing to master it. When teachers understand that they cannot force a language form upon their students, those students are more than willing to acknowledge that being "trilingual"—being as proficient in formal English and professional or technical English as they are in their "home" English—can only make them more effective.

I teach English to high school students in a large technical/ vocational high school in the Boston Public Schools. My students are fairly representative of urban American teenagers, diverse in background, low to moderate in income levels and, unfortunately, often publicly portrayed in negative ways. They are especially castigated for having low standardized test scores and poor formal English skills. In short, my classes are a good place to develop methods to help young people become proficient speakers and writers of "standard English" and for me to study the mechanics of teaching formal academic English.

In my design of lessons for my students, I have been working on the theory that there are at least three forms of the English language that most Americans need to learn in order to lead socially fulfilling and economically viable lives at this time in history:

- "home" English or dialect, which most students learn at home, and recent immigrants often learn from peers, and which for first and second generation immigrants may be a combination of English and their mother tongue
- "formal" or academic English, which is learned by many in school, from reading, and from the media, although it may also be learned in well-educated families
- "professional" English, the particular language of one's

profession, which is mostly learned in college or on the job, or, in my school, in vocational education

I think that if I can make this "trilingualism" explicit and if I can motivate students to want to learn these "languages," these three forms of English, then I can enable them to master the actual mechanical differences between them. I begin by building upon a firm respect for each student's home language—languages which, after all, are what most of us need to express connection and affection with friends and family, and what we draw upon for much of our art and cultural expression. Once this respect for home language is established, I concentrate on how different forms of English are appropriate in different contexts, instead of relying on the right/wrong dichotomy students usually face in school. I do this because I want their own usage, vocabulary, modes of expression and their self-esteem to survive the language learning process.

One result of using a right/wrong Standard English model for teaching is that it leads to many of my students saying, "Here I am in this school which tells me I'm wrong, so what do I do? Fight them all the way, stick up for my culture, resist? Or give in to the teachers and employers, in order to support my family, and live a double life, preserving a different culture at home, out of sight of those who don't understand or value me for myself?" I see no reason why students have to be convinced that the way they talk is wrong in order to master formal English grammar and speech. In fact, I find that students can learn formal grammar, complex sentence structure, scientific jargon, and many other aspects of the various forms of the language, quite fast once they discover that they can have control over the choices they make: to learn, or not learn, the languages associated with cultures in which they may decide to participate.

One way we enter this examination in my classroom is to actually study the home languages students bring into class. We find patterns of speech, rules of grammar, vocabulary, tonal features, and emotional characteristics of language which we note, label, discuss and eventually compare to the features of what we call "formal" English. I have done this successfully by asking groups of students to present the class with a good, complete description of how their members usually speak at home and with friends. I guide their preparation with the following steps:

- Come up with a name for the type of English you each speak.
- Call the class's attention to specific features of your speech by naming some of the examples of your speech, if those examples are different from formal English. Use this list for a start, giving examples of these things IF you commonly do them:

  - Failure to enunciate certain letters or sounds
  - clipped words
  - regional words or expressions (or even teenage usages)
  - slang
  - style-setting language (new, creative use of words and phrases)
  - use of other languages instead of English
  - use of other languages mixed in with English
  - double subjects
  - double negatives
  - leaving the 's' off third person singular present tense verbs
  - using the participle instead of the past tense verb
  - special tone of voice you use in special situations
  - accents or tonal features
  - use of your hands, eyes, and other "body language"
  - use of swear words, curse words or other formally "inappropriate" language (When and why do you use them, if you do?)
  - Other ways of using language that are especially interesting, creative, emotional or special in your culture or family

- Demonstrate the types of English you speak by holding a group discussion on whatever topic you like with each group member speaking his or her way.
- Prepare lots of examples of how you usually speak.
- Every member of the group must be part of the presentation to receive a grade.

I choose groups on the basis of common backgrounds whenever possible (Boston born, West Indian born, Latino, Cape Verdean, Asian background, European-American) and ask the groups to meet for an hour on each of two days to plan a presentation. I don't give them much direction, although I circulate among groups, especially if there seems to be too much gossip, not enough work, or too much confusion. I worry that they won't know what to do, but I really don't intervene much. The planning is often noisy and looks dysfunctional.

Here's a glimpse into how this project has worked. Dwayne was a member of the Boston-born group in one class. An African American seventeen-year-old whose family came from rural South Carolina, Dwayne taped an hour of his father's evening conversations with family in the kitchen, on the phone, and in front of the television. He played the tape for the class. Dwayne and the group noticed that his father tends to speak very slowly, with a musical tone which goes up and down more than an octave. Dwayne's father often clips word endings, so much so that often the class did not understand what he was saying on the tape recording, forcing Dwayne to translate. Students in Dwayne's working group noticed that Dwayne shares some of his father's speech patterns, although if they'd not heard the tape, they would not have labeled them "Southern." An interesting outgrowth of Dwayne's study of his father's speech was that he became interested in his own spelling. I think he realized that such habits as leaving the 's' off plural nouns was in some way related to his family's home language.

Juanita, a very vocal young woman who calls herself Puerto

Rican although she has lived in Boston most of her life, told the class:

> I speak English with my family, except with my grandparents. With my friends I speak English slang and sometimes Spanish. Sometimes when I speak Spanish I end up finishing my sentence in English because there is words that I don't know in Spanish.

Juanita had no trouble writing English, but felt that she needed a much larger vocabulary and a better eye for editing. She became much more willing to participate in class activities and to try harder when she encountered difficulties after doing this exercise.

Amador, a fairly recent immigrant from the Dominican Republic was asked "How long have you been in this country?"

Amador responded, "Four year."

When I asked him to say four years in Spanish, he responded, "quatro años." When I questioned him further, he said, "Every time I say that 'year,' that's a word that I know. I never heard that 's' on it."

In the discussion that followed, one student felt that it takes more time to add the 's.' Another felt that people who don't enunciate the word endings are just "lazy." One of the Spanish-background students noted that in Spanish there is usually a vowel at the end of a noun, but that in English one has to add the 's' to a consonant, which is harder to do. However, the class concluded that the "real" reason Amador didn't put an "s" on "year" was that he learned English from Americans who talk like that—that he learned English from his peers and not from his teachers.

As students study their home languages in my class, several very valuable things happen, not all of which I—or they—anticipate. One of the most wonderful for me is that I learn about their languages. While I was able to question Amador about the relationship between "four year" and "quatro años" because I have some familiarity with Spanish, and while I was able to guide

Dwayne to notice his father's "Southern" speech patterns, I have no way to anticipate difficulties that students with Vietnamese or Haitian or Russian backgrounds might have with formal English unless they teach me about their languages. For my students, the validation of their home language which comes from studying it allows them to feel comfortable with language study in general. It becomes just as acceptable to ask, "How do you say this in formal English?" as it is to ask, "How do you say this with your friends?" or, "How do you say this in your grandmother's kitchen?"

There is one obvious problem for disseminating this sort of teaching: one cannot *pretend* to respect students' home languages. If someone really felt that what certain students termed "Spanglish" or "Cringlish" or "Vietnamese-English" were really not dialects or home languages at all, but simply "broken" or "incorrect" English, they could not engage them in this type of study. If other teachers feel committed to the setting of a single "standard" for all English speech and writing in the U.S., I could not ask them to adopt these practices. However, I have found that my choice to honor these languages with formal study has been of great value in my classroom. Moreover, it has allowed us to go much further than my previous error-correction model of grammar study. We now have gone on to distinguish another form of language, the language of one's profession or trade, and we have laid the groundwork for more discoveries.

One of the ways in which the language study has led directly to chances for students to consider their language choices in life has come in our discussion of hypothetical situations in which students are likely to find themselves: job interviews, college classrooms, even the family dinner table.

Joao and Drucilla, two students whose families immigrated from Mexico, led their group in the following role-play:

Scenario: Son (played by me) returns home at Christmas from his first semester at college and his mom greets him in her own home language. College student responds in a more formal manner, using a few words his mom does not fully understand, and which sound somewhat alien to the rest of the family assembled for the holiday.

Students, playing the mother and family, had a wide variety of responses, some positive, some more negative.

In Variation I, mom responds negatively:

"You better take that mess out of this house. You're not better than nobody here."

"I am glad you are in college. But don't forget where you came from."

"Hablamos español en esta casa."

In Variation II, mom responds positively:

"I'm so proud of you talking so educated. This is why I saved money for college, and I hope the rest of you all children listen real close."

Here's another role play we tried:

Scenario: A task force has been set up at the higher level of a large business to strategize meeting stiff competition from another firm. The college student has become a junior executive, albeit one of very few from her/his race/ethnic group in the firm. This time students took all the roles.

Variation I: Our junior executive presents an advertising plan in the most formal variety of English.

Variation II: Our junior executive presents the same basic plan, but this time in her home language, or what the students in this class called "street talk."

Here are the reactions the rest of the class, who were playing the other members of the task force, had to Variation II:

- "She sounds ridiculous. Doesn't she know that doesn't play in here?"

- "Maybe if our ads were as creative as that, more people would listen to them. You know, the sneaker commercials do that."
- "It's fine for her to speak that way with her friends, but not at work."
- "I think people should respect you for your ideas, not for how you sound."

I was struck by the way that the differences of opinion became very discussable during the discussion of these role plays. Some Latino students reported that they feel more comfortable in the world if they always present themselves in formal English around non-Latino people; others felt inauthentic dropping their accent or their "Spanglish" (Pablo's term, not mine). The range of ideas and opinions on what is appropriate for each setting was very diverse and shifted as the discussion raised new issues.

I also realized that we had implanted the idea that learning a formal grammar is a choice a student makes—not a choice a teacher makes for a student. This was a real revelation to my students. Many understood that they had already made some choices in this regard, but not with the sanction and support of teachers, and not with a full and careful discussion of their options.

Patrina followed the traditional thinking about grammar learning when she wrote: "We don't hardly take time out to really listen. I mean the way we speak, we think it's correct. It's wrong, but we understand each other."

Algernon, on the other hand, saw language learning as exercising options: "[I now realize I have] the choice of speaking "formal," "slang" or both at certain times." Zaybell changed her habits: "I now listen to what I say and how I say it."

But it was Shawn who chose an even more challenging job. After writing his first long piece of prose, a fifty-page description of the trial of the man accused of murdering his brother, Shawn wrote, "What I would like to accomplish is to be able to write about something not in the least interesting. Because I want to be able to write about anything I want to write even though it may not be interesting. That's my problem. I find it so hard to work on something I dislike. So I feel if I don't get over that wall I never will."

When he entered the class, Shawn had told me that he couldn't write at all. I wish I had questioned him carefully at that time, so I would know what being able to write meant to him, and so that I might understand what happened inside him during the year. I think he began to set his own educational agenda at some point, but we certainly missed a wonderful opportunity to develop an understanding of how it happened.

As young people become less fearful of being manipulated or disrespected, I think they can become engaged in the study of their own language competence. They can weigh their options, choose how they want to speak and write in each new setting. In this atmosphere, the mechanics and usage and vocabulary of formal English no longer threaten to demean them. The study of *grammar* is very much a personal issue, a racial and class issue, a political issue—and doing it backward like this, motivation first, rules last, examining the dialects before the formal language, is something with which my students will cooperate. Further, for me the teacher, the roles of "student as expert" and "student as researcher" come a little more into focus each time we do projects like this, and as I tend to trust my students more, they in turn feel more respected and comfortable in class.

There are some new developments and some other ideas that I have yet to try. At the same time that students in my classes are studying their home languages, their peer languages, and academic English in my classroom, they are learning another set of languages in their technical classes. Although I had made some effort to examine technical or professional language with students before this, I had developed no project or systematic approach with which I was satisfied. Recently, however, my school instituted a required project in which students research and present an issue or process in their technical fields. This has given me the impetus to study professional languages with my students.

Sandra and Tracy, students in the Culinary Arts program, usually speak a very stylish and dramatic style of teenage English with their friends and in class. But in their presentation on food-borne diseases, they easily adopted an almost teacherly professional manner. The other students picked this up immediately and questioned them about it.

Sandra replied, "This is serious. You wouldn't want someone coming into your restaurant and getting sick because your staff weren't washing down the counters properly." She did not appear to feel any pressure to respond in her usual "teen talk" in this setting.

Darrell took us to the data processing lab to show us his class web page and some basic Internet surfing. He seemed very comfortable with Internet jargon, and obligingly offered explanations for his less savvy classmates. This contrasted with a certain reticence I have noticed in class. Since Darrell's speech usually contains very little "slang," I sometimes feel he speaks less to avoid being criticized for using more formal speech than his classmates. But in the presentation atmosphere, Darrell was respected for his knowledge and vocabulary and he flourished.

Kai brought the class several small animals and taught us how to feed and care for them. Kai's terminology and explanations were very precise and formal, but as with the other presentations, the class members seemed to welcome this type of language and accepted it entirely as different from ordinary class discussion.

Looking back on this use of technical language in my classroom, I notice several things. First, I realize that had I not seen the students in this other language dimension, I would not have realized how easily they moved within it or how eager they would be to do so. I probably would not have expected them to show as much respect for each other's language accomplishments as they did. Mastery of this other kind of English (for we have not settled on a name for it) is simply not threatening to my students. I am now beginning to think about the workplace as a kind of bridge for students to get to formal English, although I am just starting to think of ways to use the idea in planning lessons.

Over the next few years, I hope to listen with my students to English as it is spoken and written in all these different ways. I would like to arrange sessions where they sit in on, tape and transcribe conversations in many dialects or English variations, and then learn to analyze and compare them. I would like them to tape conversations at home and in informal classroom situations. I also hope, in cooperation with local colleges and with businesses which maintain partnerships with the school, to have students sit in on a number of other conversations in university and work environments.

My guess is that we could discover a number of useful and unexpected principles which would give us ideas for a joint plan of action to learn these "Englishes." We might possibly build a foundation for motivating each other to master the formal grammar which urban children are so criticized for not knowing. Implicit in all of this is my bet that a language barrier is part of what keeps many people "undereducated" and often poor. I am pretty sure that young people don't really understand this while they are in school, although they have inklings and the evidence surrounds them. I am convinced that high school students can achieve a deep and personal understanding of the most academic and formal varieties of English if it is separated from trappings which demean their own cultures. They still have to work harder than they are often willing to work to learn geometry and "foreign" languages and history and to write term papers, all of which are parts of the formal and professional curriculum that I think is very valuable. But I intend to explore this head-on assault on language learning and how it works in my classrooms.

CHAPTER 5

Some Basic Sociolinguistic Concepts

MICHAEL STUBBS

Like other authors in this collection, linguist MI-CHAEL STUBBS examines the relationships between language and perceptions of social class, level of education, and family background. He describes the exquisite sensitivity listeners have to the social implications of dialect and accent and the perception that speech which deviates from standard spoken English is slovenly or ugly. This is familiar territory. What is unfamiliar, however, is that Stubbs is examining these phenomena in Great Britain, where the people being stereotyped by their vernacular are those who come from Birmingham, East London, Liverpool, Newcastle, and Glasgow. Stubbs believes that children should be taught (warned of) the conventions of English, so that they can, if they wish, match their speech to the setting in which they find themselves. They should not, however, be told that their language is wrong.

There has been much debate in educational and sociological circles over the past ten or fifteen years about the precise relationship between education and language. One question often asked is: Does a child's language affect his success or failure at school? And if so, how? Many people believe that a child's language is a crucial cause of his educational success or failure. Another question often asked is: How does a teacher's language affect his pupils' learning? The aim of this chapter is to provide the reader with some basic sociolinguistic concepts necessary to understand the kinds of relationships which exist between language and educational processes. (By *sociolinguistics* I simply mean studies of how language is used in different social contexts, such as homes, factories, schools and classrooms.) Disentangling basic concepts is not merely an academic exercise, but essential to anyone who wants to understand the issues involved in the debate. What precisely is meant, for example, by the often quoted phrase: "educational failure is linguistic failure"? Does this phrase, in fact, make sense? Is there any precise meaning which can be attached to assertions that some pupils are "linguistically inadequate"? And what would constitute evidence for such assertions?

1. Language and attitudes to language

The first distinction it is crucial to be clear about is the distinction between language itself and the deeply entrenched *attitudes* and *stereotypes* which most people hold about language.

It is difficult to overestimate the importance of people's attitudes and beliefs about language. It is almost impossible, for example, to hear someone speak without immediately drawing conclusions, possibly very accurate, about his social class background, level of education and what part of the country he comes from. We hear language through a powerful filter of social values and stereotypes. As a precise example of what I mean by *linguistic stereotypes*, consider this fragment from a recorded classroom lesson which was based on a discussion of examples of dialect speech. The pupils have a transcript in front of them.

> Teacher: You can see on the bottom of your sheet, 'We ain't got no money.' That is typically a London accent—the tendency to drop the aitch off the front of words, d'you see? It's a lazy way of speaking.

Just these few comments embody several pieces of confused and dangerous linguistic folklore. The first is the *moral* censure ("lazy") which is attributed to a regional or social dialect feature. The second is the way this moral disapproval is backed up with pseudo-linguistic arguments. In the example the teacher quotes, there is nowhere to "drop an aitch" from! The teacher may mean that *ain't* is related to the standard form *haven't*. But we cannot make the form standard by saying *hain't! Ain't* is now simply a dialect form of the negative. But "dropping aitches" is a linguistic stereotype which is widely believed to characterize London speech, and it is thought to be "lazy" or "slovenly." In fact, dropping of word-initial "aitch" is found in the casual speech of educated speakers from most parts of the country. The fragment also reveals other confusions: between spoken and written language; and between "accent" or pronunciation and nonstandard grammar (e.g., the double negative). But we will leave these for the moment.

The point is that British people are very sensitive to the *social* implications of dialect and accent, and the characteristic speech of our large cities, especially Birmingham, East London, Liverpool, Newcastle and Glasgow, is often regarded as "slovenly" and "ugly." Giles (1971) carried out experiments in which people listened to standard and regional dialects. In fact they heard the same speaker using different language varieties, but they did not know this! Speakers of standard English were *perceived* as more ambitious, more intelligent, more self-confident and more reliable. Such judgements may be manifestly unfair, but it is an important *social* fact that people judge a speaker's intelligence, character and personal worth on the basis of his or her language. We ought to be aware of the power of such social stereotyping.

It has been confirmed in many other studies, and is probably obvious from everyday experience, that a speaker's language is often a major influence on our impression of his or her personality. In particular it has been shown (in a Canadian study) that teachers evaluate pupils academically on the basis of their voices, and also their physical appearance, even when they have available relevant academic work on which to form their judgements, such as written compositions and art work (Seligman et al., 1972). That is, a teacher may base serious systematic judgements about a pupil's intellectual abilities on totally irrelevant information. It is important for teachers to be aware that this tendency to linguistic stereotyping can mean that pupils may "look and sound intelligent," and therefore to be aware of the misleading clues often used in evaluating them.

As a more detailed example of the weight people often attach to superficial features of language, consider this extract from an interview I recorded with two Edinburgh schoolgirls, aged fourteen. We were discussing a tape-recording of some dialect speech.

> R: Well, they sound sort of as if they weren't very well brought up theirselves, the way they were talking.

MS: Mmhm—what are you thinking of in particular?

H: Their grammar's pretty awful.

MS: What's pretty awful about it?

H: *It only sort of went in a little bit.* (Quoting from recording.)

MS: What's wrong with that?

H: Well, you don't sort of say that, do you?

MS: Well, what in particular?

H: It's bad English.

MS: Why?

H: Well, it just sounds bad English.

MS: Which bit of it then, or is it all . . . ?

M: It only *sort* of went in.

MS: So, you don't say *sort of?*

H: I keep saying *sort of,* yeah, but you're not meant to say sort of.

MS: Well, I mean you said em *you don't sort of say that,* I think.

H: I know—you're not meant to say that sort of thing—and I know I shouldn't.

MS: Why not?

H: It just doesn't sound right. It sounds as though you're Tarzan—Me Tarzan you Jane—Me speak English—sort of—I'm saying it again, aren't I?

MS: Well, don't you think it's quite a useful expression?

H: You get into the habit of using it, I won't say it again. I'll persevere and I won't say it. You get used to saying it if you hear other people saying it—you know you sort of— I'll never do it!—you associate that sort of thing with people who haven't really been taught to say it better.

The girls interpret the language of the tape as evidence that the speakers have been badly brought up, and are not far off the level of an (intellectually?) primitive Tarzan. But, when they are pressed, all they seem to be objecting to is the use of *sort of.* This is an expression which H herself uses constantly in the extract (in spite of her efforts not to!) and which most people use in informal conversation. Again, *sort of* is a feature of language which has acquired the status of a stigmatized stereotype. What are we to think, though, of an educational system which has so tied this girl in knots over a small and superficial linguistic item?

I conducted this interview as part of a series of discussions with Edinburgh children. I asked them to listen to recordings of boys from East London, and asked them to comment on what they heard. (The children did not know where the speakers came from or who they were.) One of the most striking things was the way in which the children singled out isolated features of speech as particularly reprehensible. These included the use of *you know* and *we was*. In general, the children tended to be hyperconscious of a very few stigmatized features which were therefore made to carry a great weight of social significance. The recordings often elicited quite unjustified extrapolations like: "He sounds like a skinhead from his voice." Such is the power of linguistic stereotypes!

Some teachers might like to carry out such an experiment for themselves. It could form the topic of a lesson in English, or social science. The teacher could record people with different accents and dialects from the radio or television or from real life, and discuss with pupils why some speakers sound "posh" or "educated" or "working class," and why such judgements may be very misleading.

There is evidence that such stereotypes are transmitted at least partly by schools. Very little work has been done on institutional attitudes to language, but Milroy and Milroy (1974) have done preliminary work on teachers' attitudes to language in Northern Ireland. They have evidence that Colleges of Education are particularly sensitive to such linguistic attitudes, that they screen applicants for acceptability of speech, and that they attempt subsequently to "improve" candidates' speech. And in Glasgow, Macaulay and Trevelyan (1973) interviewed about fifty teachers. They found that almost a third of them thought that the school should try to change the way pupils speak. Some teachers implied that because some children could not use the language of the school, they were therefore less "able"—thus basing far-reaching intellectual judgements on children's speech. Such findings about teachers' attitudes to speech are, for the present, rather impressionistic, but they could be corroborated or modified by anyone reading this book from his or her own classroom observations. It would be most important, for example, to see whether comments made by teachers in interviews correspond to the way they actually attempt to modify their pupils' language in the classroom.

It is clear at any rate that schools in our society have always been very sensitive to the social meaning of different language varieties. In some extreme social situations, children have actually been forbidden to speak their own language altogether, and even punished for using their native language in schools. This has been true in the past in Britain for Welsh and Scots Gaelic speakers (Trudgill, 1974, p. 134) and in the U.S.A. for American Indian children (Hymes, 1972). These may only be extreme and explicit examples of the disapproval of children's language often found in schools today. Scots Gaelic is now used in primary schools in North West Scotland, and Welsh is actively encouraged in Welsh schools and is probably on the increase as a second language (Sharp 1973). But in the very recent past in Wales, prisoners have been forbidden to speak Welsh to visitors (*The Times*, April 28, 1972). It is important to appreciate that language differences can provoke strong feelings of language loyalty group conflict, and are therefore often a critical factor in education.

2. The primitive language myth

Having now distinguished sharply between attitudes to language and language itself, let us look at some features of languages and dialects.

It is accepted by linguists that no language or dialect is inherently superior or inferior to any other, and that all languages and dialects are suited to the needs of the community they serve. A notion that one dialect is, say, more aesthetically pleasing than another is, as we have already seen, a culturally learned notion which generally reflects the social prestige of the dialect speakers, and not inherent properties of the dialect itself. The social prestige of groups of speakers, as it were, rubs off on their language.

Linguists long ago dispelled the myth that there are primitive tribes who speak "primitive languages" with only 200–300 words, and simple grammar. It is now known that there is no correspondence at all between simplicity of material culture and simplicity of language structure, and all the world's languages have been shown to have vastly complex grammatical systems. However, the primitive language myth often lives on in a pernicious form, in the unfounded belief that the language of low income groups in rural or urban industrial areas is somehow structurally "impoverished" or "simpler" than standard English. There is no linguistic basis for such a belief. Fieldwork in urban and rural areas of Britain and the U.S.A. has demonstrated in detail that such dialects are inherently systematic and rule-governed, deeply organized systems of great complexity.

It is true, of course, that some languages are *functionally* more highly developed than others. Thus English is an international language, with a highly standardized writing system, and is used in a wide range of functions from everyday casual conversation to writing scientific papers. Many hundreds of the world's languages have no writing systems and cannot therefore serve the same range of functions. It is also clear that the native language of an Amazonian Indian is unlikely to be well suited to discuss civil engineering. It is well known that languages reflect, in the vocabulary, the needs and interests of their speakers.

None of these points, however, affect the central issue that all languages and dialects are vastly complex structural systems.

3. Standard and nonstandard dialects

I have already used terms such as "standard language" and "dialect" without discussing what they mean. Such terms are in common usage and although people usually think they know what they mean, the terms turn out to be rather elusive. It is important to be precise about them, however, since the aspect of language variation which a teacher is likely to come up against most often in the classroom is a pupil who speaks "nonstandard" English.

The term *dialect* is in everyday usage, meaning the language variety used in a particular geographical region or by a particular social class group. Linguists often distinguish between *regional* and *social dialects*. In theory these might be distinct, but in Britain the regional and social dimensions are related. Briefly, the higher up the social class scale one goes, the less one encounters regional variation in speech. This is one reason why British people are so sensitive to the social implications of the kind of language a speaker uses. Thus educated people in the upper middle class all over Britain speak in very much the same way, allowing for minor differences in pronunciation. But farm workers, say, from Devon and Aberdeen might have considerable difficulties in understanding each other.

The term *standard English* is used in several partly contradictory ways. It is sometimes taken to mean the social dialect of the educated class in Britain (which developed historically from the prestige regional dialect of certain London speakers). But this standard turns out to be rather hard to pin down, since it has nowhere been described in detail. Such a definition is, in any case, circular: it asserts that standard English is the English spoken by educated people, and that what they speak is standard English. A different notion of standard English is the language which is partially codified in dictionaries, grammar books and manuals of good usage. But this English is often a codification of norms of *written* English, and often only loosely related to how English is *spoken*. There is often confusion, then, about whether standard English corresponds to the way a certain social group actually speaks, or to a prescriptive ideal which states how we *ought* to speak (or write). Given this confusion over standard English, it is not surprising to find that the standard transmitted by schools is often a mixture of local prejudice about what is a "good accent," sometimes outdated notions of educated usage and notions of written, or even literary, language which may be quite inappropriate to speech.

Note also that we have to distinguish between *accent* (or pronunciation) and *dialect*. My own speech, for example, might be described as standard English with a regional West of Scotland accent. There is, in fact, no standard English accent, and standard English may be spoken with any accent.

Given the lack of a precise definition for standard English, it is even more difficult to say what is meant by "nonstandard" English, although this term is widely used. How much must a variety deviate from the "standard" before it is labelled "nonstandard"? In view of the accent/dialect distinction, we might want to say that it has to deviate more than in terms of pronunciation alone. But if we compare standard and nonstandard dialects in terms of grammar and vocabulary, we will find only relatively minor variations across the country. Local words and expressions, for example, form only a very small percentage of most people's usage.

We can safely leave linguists to worry over the problems of defining the precise line of demarcation between languages and dialects. The point at issue is that such differences, although often small and not clearcut, are often the focus for powerful feelings of group loyalty and for far-reaching social judgements on speakers. We find, for example, that people are often hypersensitive to the social implications of dialect forms like *we was* and *we ain't*. Yet from a linguistic point of view such forms are neither superior or inferior to standard forms: they do not, for example, cause any ambiguity in meaning. Schools in particular have traditionally been very sensitive to such aspects of language, and have often seen it as one of their functions to disseminate the standard language.

Language varieties

Different language is used in different situations, so we can say that a language is not a uniform object. It is a basic principle of sociolinguistics that there are no single-style speakers (Labov 1970). That is, everyone is multidialectal or multistylistic, in the sense that he adapts his style of speaking to suit the social situation in which he finds himself. It is intuitively clear, for example, that a boy does not speak in the same way to his teachers, his parents, his girlfriend or his friends in the playground. Imagine the disastrous consequences all round if he did! His way of talking to his teacher will also change according to the topic: answering questions in class or organizing the school sports. People adapt their speech according to the person they are talking to and the point behind the talk. These are social rather than purely linguistic constraints.

As a more general example of what I have in mind by language varieties, consider the following rather mixed bag of different varieties or styles of English, spoken and written: BBC English, Cockney, officialese, journalese, lecture, church sermon. These language varieties differ along several dimensions, notably regional/geographical, social class, and functional/contextual. But their description involves questions of the same order: Who says what? To whom? When? Where? Why? and How? In addition, more than one dimension is typically involved in any one of the varieties. For example, "BBC English" implies not only that the speaker is likely to come from a certain region (southern Britain) and belong to a certain social class (educated middle class), but also implies a relatively formal social situation (probably not casual conversation in a pub). Some of what I have listed as language varieties might be thought of rather as speech situations. But speech and situation are not entirely separable in this way. For example, it is not simply that certain social situations demand that a teacher "gives a pupil a dressing down." By "giving a pupil a dressing down" the teacher may create a certain social situation! Note the importance of the concept of language variation when discussing children's language. A teacher may tend to think of a child's language in a stereotyped way, as though the child was a one-variety speaker. But the teacher typically sees the child in only a narrow range of social situations in the classroom, and may forget that the child also controls *other* language varieties. In other words, many teachers are unaware that all speech communities use ranges of different language varieties in different social contexts; yet this is an elementary sociolinguistic fact. Conversely, many teachers maintain the fiction that there is only one "best" English for all purposes, and that this is the only English proper to the classroom. Yet a moment's thought or observation will convince any teachers that they themselves use many varieties of language throughout the day, depending on the purpose or context of the communication. This is not reprehensible, implying a chameleon-like fickleness, but a basic sociolinguistic fact about language use all over the world.

Correctness or appropriateness?

The concept that different language varieties are suited to different situations can be summed up in the distinction which is often drawn between correctness and appropriateness of language. Many of us were taught at school some version of the doctrine of correctness: that "good English" means grammatically correct standard English; and that the use of colloquialisms, slang or non-standard forms is "bad English." No linguist would nowadays take this *prescriptive* attitude. Contemporary linguistics is strictly *descriptive*: it describes what people do, and does not try to prescribe what they ought to do. This does not mean, of course, that "anything goes." If a pupil writes a letter to a prospective employer which is full of colloquialisms or nonstandard forms, he will have to be warned of the conventions of English usage. It is not that such forms are wrong in any absolute sense, but that they are considered inappropriate to this social occasion: applying for a job.

Macaulay and Trevelyan (1973) interviewed personnel managers, a careers officer and the director of an employment agency in Glasgow, to investigate the importance employers attach to speech in interviewing school leavers for jobs. They discovered that most employers feel that speech is important and may be crucial at the interview stage. Only a few of those interviewed said that an applicant's accent was important, but there were many complaints about "slovenly speech." There is no reason why such views about language should not be discussed openly with pupils in schools: in the English classroom, for example. As Macaulay and Trevelyan say, social judgements about language, particularly about accent, are "treated as a taboo subject even less mentionable than sex or money."

To say that a piece of language is "wrong" is therefore to make a judgement relative to a social situation. It may be felt just as inappropriate to use colloquialisms and regional dialect forms in a job interview, as it is to use very formal language over a drink with some friends in a pub. In the first instance one is likely to be thought uncouth, impolite, socially gauche or uneducated. (However unjustified such judgements may be, it is only fair to warn pupils that people *do* base harsh social judgements on surface characteristics of other people's speech. The ultimate aim here must be to make more people more tolerant of linguistic diversity.) In the second case one risks being thought aloof, stand-offish, "lah-de-dah" or a bit of a snob.

It follows, then, that *within* standard English—and any other dialect, of course—there is stylistic variation according to social context. Thus standard English has formal and informal styles in both writing and speech. So, the use of colloquial forms, slang or swear words are all quite normal *within* standard English. They simply define the style as informal: they do not define it as non-standard. As a speaker of standard English moves between different social situations, he or she will *style-shift*. But precisely the same functions may be served by other speakers shifting between dialects. For example, many West Indian children in Britain are *bi-*

dialectal, between a form of Creole English used in the home and a more formal language variety, much closer to standard English, used in school.

A teacher may often find that he wants both to defend some controversial form (e.g., split infinitives) because it is nowadays in widespread usage, but also to warn pupils not to use it when, say, writing a job application. In other words, the question "What is correct English?" is too oversimple to answer. (Mittins, 1969, gives an entertaining and sensible discussion of this.) To say therefore, that someone's English is "wrong" is to make not a linguistic, but a *sociolinguistic* judgement.

Production and comprehension

Suppose then that a teacher observes that a child uses language which is inappropriate (in the teacher's terms) for the classroom. Is this because the child does not know the forms the teacher thinks appropriate? Or because the child knows the forms but does not realize that it is appropriate to use them in this situation? If a teacher observes that a child never *produces* a particular linguistic item (word, sentence-type, etc.) this may mean several things: (a) that the child neither knows nor understands the item; (b) that the child *understands* the item, but never *uses* it in his own speech; or (c) that the child both knows and uses the item, but the teacher has never observed the child in a situation where the child finds it appropriate and necessary to use it. We all have a passive knowledge of many aspects of our language, words and constructions, which we understand but never actively use. An adult's passive vocabulary, for example, typically includes several hundred words which he understands but does not use. And most of us can understand certain styles of language, say the language of the courtroom, which we could not, however, competently use ourselves. Similarly, young children understand many things that their parents say to them long before they can actively produce the same items. That is, speakers have asymmetrical linguistic systems: they can perceive and understand linguistic distinctions which they do not (or cannot) themselves make.

A simple experiment by Labov (1969) illustrates this distinction sharply. He asked Negro youths in the U.S.A. who were speakers of nonstandard dialect simply to repeat the sentence: "I asked Alvin if he knows how to play basketball." The boys were unable to repeat this standard English sentence, and instead regularly produced a nonstandard sentence such as "I axt Alvin does he know how to play basketball." That is, they produced a version which differed from the original in details of surface grammar. Clearly, the boys had *understood* the *meaning* of the original sentence, since they could immediately and correctly translate the sentence into their own dialect. Yet they could not *produce* the surface grammar of the target sentence. We must therefore be very careful before we equate the inability to *use* a particular grammatical form with the inability to *understand* it or the concept which underlies it. . . .

5. The implication of such distinctions

These distinctions between different aspects of linguistic competence are not merely academic. They show at once that any claim to relate "language" directly to "education" is almost certain to be so oversimple as to be meaningless. Is one talking about: comprehension or production? language structure or language use? prescriptive norms of correctness or appropriateness to social context? grammatical or communicative competence? the child's language itself or the school's attitudes to his language? It should already be clear how oversimple it is to say that a child's language *directly* determines his success or failure at school. The child uses different *varieties* of language in different *social situations*, say home and school. The teacher may (rightly or wrongly) regard the child's language as *inappropriate* to the classroom. The child's language may also provoke negative *attitudes* in the teacher, perhaps because the child speaks a low prestige dialect. These attitudes may be transmitted to the child. Even if the teacher expresses no overt disapproval of the child's language, the teacher's own language may still be different from the child's in the direction of prestige varieties, and this in itself may be an implicit condemnation of the child's language. The child will be aware that people with more prestige and authority than him speak differently, and may draw his own conclusions. Such a complex of sociolinguistic factors may lead cumulatively to educational problems for a child.

Thus a child's language may be a *disadvantage* in his educational progress: not because his language is itself "deficient," but because it is different. These distinctions may seem initially to recall the Feiffer cartoon which runs:

> I used to think I was poor. Then they told me I wasn't poor, I was *needy*. Then they told me it was self-defeating to think of myself as needy, I was *deprived*. Then they told me deprived was a bad image. I was *underprivileged*. Then they told me underprivileged was overused. I was *disadvantaged*. I still haven't got a dime, but I have a great vocabulary.

But it is important to ask just how the disadvantage arises. Is it "in" children's language? Or does it arise rather from people's attitudes to language differences? If you believe that children's language can be "deficient," then you might be tempted to try and improve their language in some way. If you believe on the contrary that the concept of language deficit does not make much sense, and that there is nothing wrong with the language of any normal child, then you will probably believe that schooling should not interfere with children's dialects. And if you believe that linguistic disadvantage arises largely from people's intolerance and prejudice towards language differences, then you will probably try to change people's attitudes to language.

REFERENCES AND NAME INDEX

Atkinson, P. (1975). In cold blood: bedside teaching in a medical school. In Chanan and Delamont (eds.).

Barnes, D. (1971). Language and learning in the classroom. *Journal of Curriculum Studies 3*, I.

———— (1969). *Language in the secondary classroom*. In Barnes et al.

———— et al. (1969). *Language, the Learner and the School*. Harmondsworth: Penguin.

———— and Todd, F. (1975). *Communication and Learning in Small Groups*. Report to SSRC, Mimeo.

Bellack, A. (ed.) (1973). *Studies in the Classroom Language*. New York: Teachers College Press.

———— et al. (1966). *The Language of the Classroom*. New York: Teachers College Press.

Bernstein, B. (ed.) (1971, 1972, 1975). *Class, Codes and Control* Vols. I, 2, and 3. London: Routledge & Kegan Paul.

———— (1971). On the classification and framing of educational knowledge. In Young (ed.).

Boggs, S. T. (1972). The meaning of questions and narratives to Hawaian children. In Cazden et al. (eds.).

Brumfit, C. J. and Reeder, K. F. (1974). The role of language study in teacher education. *Educational Review* 26, 3.

Cazden, C., John, V., Hymes, D. (eds.) (1972). *Functions of Language in the Classroom*. New York: Teachers College Press.

Chanan, G. and Delamont, S. (eds.) (1975). *Frontiers of Classroom Research*. Slough: NFER.

Creber, P. (1972). *Lost for Words*. Harmondsworth: Penguin.

Delamont, S. (1976). *Interaction in the Classroom*. London: Methuen.

Delamont, S. and Hamilton, D. (1976). Classroom research: a critique and a new approach. In Stubbs and Delamont (eds.).

Dumont, R. V. (1972). Learning English and how to be silent: studies in Sioux and Cherokee classrooms. In Cazden et al. (eds.).

Flanders, N. (1970). *Analyzing Teaching Behaviour.* London: Addison-Wesley.

Flower, F. D. (1966). *Language and Education.* London: Longman.

Furlong, V. (1976). Interaction sets in the classroom: towards a study of pupil knowledge. In Stubbs and Delamont (eds.).

Gannaway, H. (1976). Making sense of school. In Stubbs and Delamont (eds.).

Giles, H. (1971). Our reactions to accent. *New Society*, 14 October.

Greene, J. (1975). *Thinking and Language.* London: Methuen (Essential Psychology series).

Gumperz, J. J. and Herasimchuk, E. (1972). The conversational analysis of social meaning: a study of classroom interaction. In R. Shuy (ed.). *Sociolinguistics*, Georgetown Monograph Series on Language and Linguistics, 25.

Hall, R. A. Jr. (1972). Pidgins and creoles as standard languages. In Pride and Holmes (eds.).

Hamilton, D. (1976). The advent of curriculum integration: paradigm lost or paradigm regained? In Stubbs and Delamont (eds.).

——— (1971). The genesis of classroom research as a legitimate field of educational research. Paper read to Conference on Classroom Observation, Lancaster, PA.

Hammersley, M. (1974). The organization of pupil participation. *Sociological Review*, August.

Hawkins, P. (1969). Social class, the nominal group and reference. In Bernstein (ed.) (1972).

Herriot, P. (1971). *Language and Teaching.* London: Methuen.

Hess, R. D. and Shipman, V. C. (1965). Early experience and the socialization of cognitive modes in children. In A. Cashdan and E. Grudgeon (eds.) (1972). *Language in Education.* London: Routledge & Kegan Paul.

HMSO (1975). *A Language for Life*. Report of the Bullock Committee.

Hocrker, J. and Ahlbrandt, P. A. (1969). The persistence of recitation. *American Educational Research Journal 6*, 2.

Hymes, D. (1967). Models of the interaction of language and social setting. *Journal of Social Issues*.

———— (1972). Introduction. In Cazden *et al.* (eds.).

Jackson, L. A. (1974). The myth of elaborated and restricted code. *Higher Education Review 6*, 2.

Jackson, P. W. (1968). *Life in Classrooms*. New York: Holt, Rinehart & Winston.

Keddie, N. (1971). Classroom knowledge. In Young (ed.).

———— (ed.) (1973). *Tinker, Tailor... The Myth of Cultural Deprivation*. Harmondsworth: Penguin.

Kochman, T. (1972). Black American speech events and a language programme for the classroom. In Cazden et al. (eds.).

Labov, W. (1966). *The Social Stratification of English in New York City*. Washington: Center for Applied Linguistics.

———— (1969). The logic of nonstandard English. In Keddic (ed.).

———— (1969b). Some sources of reading problems for Negro speakers of nonstandard English. In J. C. Baratz and R. Shuy (eds.) *Teaching Black Children to Read*. Washington: Center for Applied Linguistics.

———— (1970). The study of language in a social context. *Studium Generale 23*, 1. Excerpt in Pride and Holmes (eds.).

———— (1972). Rules for ritual insults. In D. Sudnow (ed.) *Studies in Social Interaction*. Glencoe: Free Press.

———— (1973). The linguistic consequences of being a lame. *Language in Society 2*, 1.

Lambert, W. E. (1967). A social psychology of bilingualism. In Pride and Holmes (eds.).

Lee, V. (1973). *Social Relationships and Language*. Buckinghamshire: Open University Press.

Macaulay, R., and Trevelyan, G. (1973). *Language, Education and Employment in Glasgow*. Report to SSRC, Mimeo.

Medley, D. M. and Mitzel, H. E. (1963). Measuring classroom behaviour by systematic observation. In N. L. Gage (ed.) *Handbook of Research on Teaching*. Chicago: Rand McNally.

Mehan, H. (1973). Assessing children's school performance. In H. P. Dreitzel (ed.) *Childhood and Socialization*, Recent Sociology 5. London: Macmillan.

Mehrabian, A. (1968). Inference of attitudes from the posture, orientation and distance of a communicator. In M. Argyle (ed.) (1973). *Social Encounters*. Harmondsworth: Penguin.

Milroy, J., and Milroy, A. L. (1974). A sociolinguistic project in Belfast. Queen's University Belfast, Mimeo.

Mishler, E. (1972). Implications of teacher-strategies for language and cognition: observations in first-grade classrooms. In Cazden et al, (eds.).

Mitchell-Kernan, C. (1972). On the status of Black English for native speakers: an assessment of attitudes and values. In Cazden et al. (eds.).

Mittins, W. H. (1969). What is correctness? *Educational Review* 22, 1.

Nuthall, G. A. (1968). A review of some selected recent studies of classroom interaction and teaching behaviour. In J. Gallagher et al. *Classroom Observation*. Chicago: Rand McNally.

Philips, S. (1972). Participant structures and communicative competence: Warm Springs children in community and classroom. In Cazden et al. (eds.).

Postman, N. and Weingartner, C. (1969). *Teaching as a Subversive Activity*. Harmondsworth: Penguin.

Pride, J. and Holmes, J. (eds.) (1972). *Sociolinguistics*. Harmondsworth: Penguin.

Rosen, H. (1973). *Language and Class: A Critical Look at the Theories of Basil Bernstein*. Bristol: Falling Wall Press.

Rosenthal, R. and Jacobson, L. (1968). *Pygmalion in the Classroom*. New York: Holt, Rinehart & Winston.

Seligman, C. R., et al. (1972). The effects of speech style and other attributes on teachers' attitudes toward children. *Language in Society I* 1.

Sharp, D. (1973). *Language in Bilingual Communities*. London: Edward Arnold.

Simon, A. and Boyer, E. B. (eds.) (1967, 1970). *Mirrors for Behaviour.* Philadelphia: Research for Better Schools.

Sinclair, J. M. (1973). English for effect. *Commonwealth Education Liason Committee Newsletter 3*, 11.

Sinclair, J. M. and Coulthard, R. M. (1974). *Towards an Analysis of Discourse: The English Used by Teachers and Pupils.* London: Oxford University Press.

Snyder, B. (1971). *The Hidden Curriculum.* New York: Knopf.

Stubbs, M. (1976). Keeping in touch: some functions of teacher-talk. In Stubbs and Delamont (eds.).

——— (1975). Teaching and talking: a sociolinguistic approach to classroom interaction. In Chanan and Delamont (eds.).

———, and Delamont, S. (eds.) (1976). *Explorations in Classroom Observation.* London: Wiley.

Torode, B. (1976). Teacher's talk and classroom discipline. In Stubbs and Delamont (eds.).

Trudgill, P. (1975). *Accent, Dialect and the School.* London: Edward Arnold.

——— (1975b). Review of B. Bernstein *Class, Codes and Control*, Vol I. *Journal of Linguistics 11*, 1.

——— (1974). *Sociolinguistics.* Harmondsworth: Penguin.

Turner, G. J. (1973). Social class and children's language of control at age 5 and age 7. In Bernstein (ed.), Vol. 2.

Walker, R. and Adelman, C. (1976). Strawberries. In Stubbs and Delamont (eds.).

——— (1975). *A Guide to Classroom Observation.* London: Methuen.

——— (1975b). Interaction analysis in informal classrooms: a crucial comment on the Flanders system. *British Journal of Educational Psychology 45*, 1.

——— (1972). *Towards a Sociography of the Classroom.* Report to SSRC, Mimeo.

Wight, J. (1971). Dialect in school. *Educational Review 24*, I.

———— (1975). Language through the looking glass. *Ideas*, Curriculum Magazine, Goldsmiths College, London, 31.

————, and Norris, R. (1970). *Teaching English to West Indian Children.* Schools Council Working Paper 29. London: Methuen.

Wilkinson, A. (1971). *The Foundations of Language*. London: Oxford University Press.

Young, M.F.D. (ed.) (1971). *Knowledge and Control*. London: Collier-Macmillan.

CHAPTER 6

Language, Culture, and the Assessment of African American Children

ASA G. HILLIARD III

Because teaching and learning are rooted in environments that are shaped by politics, says psychologist and historian ASA HILLIARD, educational assessments of African American children cannot be divorced from the historically oppressed status of African Americans in the United States. Hilliard dismantles the notion that African American culture is an insufficient reflection of Western culture, or that Ebonics is an inadequate attempt at Standard English. Instead, he provides a picture of the richness of the culture and language, not only as independent entities, but as major contributors to larger American society. He urges us to produce educators who can examine the big picture behind an education system that assesses not a child's aptitude for learning, but which words she speaks.

Teaching and learning are rooted in and are dependent upon a common language between teacher and student. Language is rooted in and is an aspect of culture. Culture is nothing, more nor less, than the shared ways that groups of people have created to use and define their environment. All people, every group of people on the face of the Earth, have created culture. Therefore, they have also created language, which is included in culture. Children all over the world learn to speak the language of their cultural group at about the age of two. Teaching and learning is a worldwide phenomenon. The teaching function and the learning function have occurred in every culture on Earth. It is natural and not the exclusive property of any group or groups. Teaching and learning—the transmission of cultural heritage—is as old as the human family. All cultures are intellectually complicated and cognitively demanding.

Teaching and learning are also rooted in environments that are shaped by politics. For example, the United States was created as a slave nation, complete with deliberate designs to prevent the education of slaves. The designs included measures that would create certain beliefs to justify that curtailment. For example, the belief in and the ideology of white supremacy have led to the development of an ideology that says that genetically, whites are intellectually superior and people of color inferior. This thinking has resulted in a greater segregation of students in schools and disproportionate placement of people of color in certain categories of special education (College Board 1985; Goodlad 1984; Guthrie 1979; Hilliard 1990, 1996; Oakes and Lipton 1990).

A review of the documents shows just how pervasive was the influence of such academic disciplines as history, geography, religion, biology, psychology, anthropology, sociology, and linguistics in the creation and teaching of racist beliefs (Carter and Goodwin 1994; Chase 1977; Kamin 1974). The legacy of these beliefs remains with us today, often wearing the cloak of scientific legitimacy. Africans were said by some historians to have had no history, by linguists to have had inferior language, by political scientists to have had poor self-government, by psychologists to have had low intelligence, by biologists to have had inferior genes, and by theologians to have had no soul—among other things (Guthrie 1976; Hegel 1831; Turner 1969). These views were enshrined in scientific literature of recent decades. They were taught in universities and colleges. And so, through no fault of the slaves, unprovoked, systematic, and pervasive oppression was instituted and maintained with the help of those many in education who were most responsible for freedom (Anderson 1988; King 1971; Spivey 1978).

Language, Culture, Oppression, and African Americans

And so, we have before us today culture and pedagogy issues, one of which is the issue of culture and assessment. Valid assessment is thought to be a part of the design of valid pedagogy; yet this is a culturally plural society with political problems based on culture. That issue must be handled in terms of a total context. Language, culture, history, and oppression are inextricably linked together where African American children are concerned. To attempt to analyze assessment practice by reference to language or culture alone will doom such analyses to failure. Indeed, it might well result in data that support beliefs and behaviors which would make matters worse than they already are for African American children.

It is the purpose of this essay to identify certain important language issues and to suggest prerequisites for the constructs of valid assessment.

It cannot be denied that African American children are not achieving at optimal levels in the schools of the nation. Neither can it be denied that there is a need for African American children to learn languages and content other than that which many have already learned up to now. The real problem we are forced to confront is this: Can we be explicit about how professional practice can be made to perform the normal and expected function of facilitating the natural healthy learning processes of children? In particular, how can the assessment process be purified so as to operate in the service of African American children rather than against them?

I speak of African American children and not "minority," "at risk," "disadvantaged," "culturally or otherwise deprived," or even "Black," except as it is equivalent in meaning to African American. The reasons for this are scientific rather than either ideological or political. Of the terms above, only "African American" suggests the need to refer to children's *antecedents, ethnicity,* and *cultural environmental experiences* for explanations and interpretations of a group of people. For example, what are the historical antecedents of a "minority"? I intend to show that it is the failure of scholarship to take history and culture into account that distorts scientific study. Failing to deal with the existence of oppression and its impact will result in a further distortion of study.

Perhaps it is the limited cultural experience of so many U.S. scholars that renders cultural data "invisible." Perhaps at a deeper level there is some white guilt about racial oppression, including oppression through the invalid use of tests, and a sense of impotence to change the systems that serve those ends at the base of the problem of how to make the healthy and normal experiences of African Americans visible to investigators, without the typical retreat to assumptions of pathology among the children. For many years now, there are those of us who have charged that mass-produced standardized professional tests and materials are ill suited to the needs of most African American children, in part because certain false assumptions are made about the children and their culture. Basically, the erroneous core assumption is that African American children are nothing more than incomplete copies of Western European white children. When it is recognized that African American children have a unique culture, that culture is usually seen as inferior to the Western European culture. It is these general ideas that cause gross errors to be made in testing and assessment in four areas in particular:

1. in testing the "mental ability" of African American children
2. in testing the speech of African American children
3. in testing the language of African American children
4. in testing the reading ability of African American children.

These errors are made because most professionals are ignorant of certain basic linguistic principles and of the history of American English and African American speech (Cohen 1969; D'Andrade 1995; Hilliard 1983; Hoover, Politzer and Taylor 1995; Shuy 1977). Therefore, professionals make mistakes when dealing both with English and with African English. Let's look at this more closely.

Misconceptions About Common American English

1. English is immaculately conceived and is a pure language.
2. English is superior to other languages.
3. English is a fixed or permanent language.
4. English is essentially the same in all English-speaking countries and in the United States.
5. English in America is uninfluenced by African language.
6. English is language, not simply a language.

The President's Commission on Foreign Language Study has already sounded the alarm about the poor language preparation of Americans and about the poor attitudes Americans display toward other languages. Few Americans have been taught such simple things as how English really came to be. Were its true evolution widely known, chauvinistic attitudes toward language might be dismantled.

According to Fromkin and Rodman (1993), Romans invaded Britain in the first century A.D. and dominated Germanic Celts, the previous conquerors of Britain. Britain's northern tribes, the Scots and Picts, were attacking the Celtic invaders at the time that Romans arrived, but Rome prevailed. And as the power of Rome declined during the fifth century, the Romans left Britain. The Celts then sent for Germanic Jutes (Teuton mercenaries) to repel their old enemies, the Scots and the Picts. In 449 A.D., the Jutes helped to defeat the Scots and the Picts and having won, decided to dominate their cousins the Celts with the help of other Germanic tribes, and the Angles and Saxons. It is from the Angles and Saxons and the linguistic soup already present in the British Isles that English was born.

Meanwhile, the Celts left for Wales, Cornwall, and France, and themselves began to speak Welsh, Scottish, Gaelic, and Breton. For the next six hundred years or so, English, as spoken by the Germanic conquerors of Britain at varying times, evolves, even as the German spoken in Germany continues to evolve to the point where emerging English and German, one of its parent languages, are no longer mutually intelligible. (Franklin and Rodman 1993)

In 1066, William the Conqueror invaded and conquered Britain and established French as the national language. English was still the language of the masses, but it was influenced by French. By 1500, British English began to be quite similar to the English that is spoken in England today. And so, what is now English emerged as a polyglot language from the remnants of the language of Celts, Latins, Germanic Jutes, Angles, Saxons, and finally the French.

The result is a language that is largely Germanic in grammar and largely Romance in vocabulary. In fact, we could with some merit argue that English is "nonstandard German." This is hardly a pure or immaculately conceived language, nor is it permanent or fixed. It would be difficult to demonstrate its superiority to any other language. Indeed, it was the linguist and scientist Benjamin Whorf who observed after learning the Hopi Indian language that it was more suitable for sophisticated scientific thought than was his native English. We will deal with the African influence later.

What we are left with, then, is that English, common American English, is simply a language of convenience. As a common language, it is efficient for the nation. Yet, the approach to teaching English in our schools seeks to establish standards for aesthetics and to establish a national cultural heritage based on it. Instead of thinking of "standard" as common or ordinary, "standard English" is thought of as a standard of quality. The effect of this thinking is to subordinate any alternative and to label that alternative as inferior.

Misconceptions About African American Language

To refer to the language of most African Americans as "nonstandard English" is to mislead people, since the implication is that all that is involved is a variant of English. And yet, like English, the language spoken by African Americans is a fusion of languages *that cannot be understood apart from an appeal to historical origins and to the oppression of slavery*. Winifred Vass (1974) has shown that about 49.1 percent of the Africans who were enslaved were sent to South America, and 42.2 percent were sent to the Caribbean and to the Greater and Lesser Antilles. About 1.8 percent were sent to Europe and its island environs. The remainder, about 6.8 percent, went to the United States, Mexico, Canada, and Central America. It is important to know that the 4.5 percent of the total trade that came to the United States came mostly during the last fifty years of the slave trade, when by the end of the slave trade, West Africa had been heavily depopulated. Therefore, Africans were brought to the United States from Angola, with many Africans coming through Angola from as far away as Mozambique and South East Africa on the coast. Thus, during the heaviest years of African enslavement in the U.S., the primary source of people was from the core band of Bantu language culture, and the Africans

who were brought to the United States were speakers of one or
more of the Bantu languages. Further, one of the principal features
of the Bantu family of languages is that they covered the largest
part of the African continent. In addition, a well-known characteristic of Bantu languages is something that those who know them
have called the "Bantu dynamic." That is to say, these languages
exert a powerful influence on other languages. They tend to have
tenacity and staying power. It is the retention of the "Bantu dynamic" that is picked up by Lorenzo Turner (1969), who showed
how features of African languages, far from being lost during enslavement, were retained in the speech of the Sea Islanders in
South Carolina.

Winifred K., a resident of Zaire for over forty years and fluent
in Tshiluba, a Bantu language, has described the Bantu dynamic:

> The cultural picture of the Bantu emphasizes a strong oral
> tradition which places supreme ethnographic value on an in-
> dividual's ability to communicate impressively. The conquer-
> ing process begun by metal spears was continued by a gift of
> speech so forceful that it was adopted by successive ethnic
> groups, which continued to exist as separate cultural and
> physical entities within the total Bantu pattern. The Bantu
> speech dynamic has asserted itself in a new setting, transported
> to this continent by Bantu-speaking slaves. The Afro-American
> has retained the deft canny power of communications which
> has enabled him to "use language in the contexts of the sit-
> uations," to "manipulate and control situations to give him-
> self the winning edge" (Vass 1974: 102).

As Vass has shown, this Bantu dynamic is not limited in its impact
to the African continent. In fact, the most highly visible oral culture in America today is the speech of lower-class African Americans.

Today, Africans and African Americans are a race of gifted
speakers, though the motives for unexcelled speech performance
have changed from the motive of sheer physical survival to motives

expressing the deep psychological needs of the human personality. Completely uninhibited in his efforts to imitate a strange speech, the Bantu-speaking slave brought from Africa had the inner will to expression and the sensitivity to the human situation which furnish the basis for the greatest potential that every African American has today, his own personal share of the Bantu past. Conscious of it or not, black and white Americans are the inheritors today of a rich cultural contribution: the tough, lusty, good-natured, and uncannily perceptive part of our speech which is our Bantu heritage (Vass 1974: 103).

Vass documents the Bantu retention in the speech of both black and white Southerners. She identifies the names of many southern cities today that are Bantu in origin and also locates many Bantu words in the vocabulary of Southerners. She decodes such familiar songs as "Polly Wolly Doodle" and "Here We Go Loop de Loop," which are shown to be freedom songs that are from the Bantu (see also Alleyne 1971; Turner 1969).

Having lived in West Africa for six years, I can attest to a similar dynamic among people there. Liberia is a West African nation of 26 languages, virtually all a part of the Bantu family of languages. It is a common saying in Liberia, "Never let a Liberian man talk for himself in court. If you do, you will lose." I am witness to the fact that it is common for young children to rec-ognize and speak two or more African languages and some English as well. I saw no evidence that "large lips and tongues," as early linguists had said, "were physical impediments to speech" (Turner 1969:6). I saw no evidence of genetic or linguistic inferiority over the time spent in Liberia. I did find a strong oral culture where even young children are frequently excellent public speakers. These examples in Liberia of a powerful oral language, like that described by Vass, show the Bantu dynamic in action, the power of speech exhibited. It is clear that early linguists spoke out of their own ignorance of African language and culture, much the same as many did and still do about the language of African Amer-icans.

The historical, political, and cultural information is important when we learn that many of the things which cause African American children to be labeled as "poor readers," "dumb" (low intelligence), or as "speech impaired" are the retained features of Bantu speech or speech from other African language families mixed with or fused into a form of common English (Alleyne 1971; Turner 1969; Vass 1974). Ironically, some varieties of common English— i.e., white Southern speech—also are influenced by the Bantu dynamic. It is important to note that the African retention in the language of African Americans covers all the features that go to make up language—i.e., vocabulary, phonology, grammar, etc. (Smith 1978).

So, it should be clear that we are really talking about two amalgams when we speak of English and African American speech. To realize this is to reduce the professional problem considerably. The language spoken by many African Americans should simply be regarded as a "foreign" or "semi-foreign" language and not as "pathological" or "deficient." The prime test of the "normalcy" of the language of a child is to compare the child's language to the environment within which it was learned. This simple test seems to have been overlooked by many test makers and linguists alike.

From the minimal information presented above, it should be clear that any linguists or other students of the language of African Americans will have serious deficiencies in their professional preparation if they are ignorant of the African cultural linguistic antecedents.

The Practical Consequences of a Reorientation

Much of the language and many constructs in testing and assessment must be redefined or eliminated! These assessment practices are inconsistent and incompatible with and contradictory to valid cultural-linguistic principles (Rowe 1991; Salomon 1995). Yet testing and assessment, as we now see them in education, are rooted in and dependent upon language.

Let's take a look at some constructs that will prove to be absurd under the light of cultural-linguistics analysis:

- "basic word" list
- word "difficulty"
- "vocabulary"
- "general information"
- standardized "beginning and ending sounds"
- standardized "comprehension"

Standardized test makers assume that there is, in general, a unique correct answer to a given question or problem. If there is not a unique answer, if there can be multiple answers, then the scoring and analysis system disintegrates. This matter is fundamental! What I am asserting is a basic threat not only to biased testing and assessment of African American children, but to the very foundation of testing and assessment for any child. The results of standardized testing favor children who speak common American English simply because these children are able to respond to questions that are couched in a familiar language based upon familiar experiences. Since the "right children"—upper class, wealthy—tend to get the top scores, it is assumed that the I.Q., reading, speech, language acquisition, and other tests are valid. Test makers have no way of taking the achievement results of a privileged child and separating that part of the scores which is due to the student's special skill and that part which is due simply to growing up in the common white American culture. Because the results come out "right" or appear to have "face validity," the basic assumptions about what the testing and assessment process is supposed to be doing are left unexamined. Let's look at this more closely:

What are the criteria for the establishment of a "basic word list"? Is a basic word list something that all Americans can be expected to have had an equally likely chance to encounter? Is a basic word list a random sample of vocabulary from the total possible vocabulary pool? Does a basic word list represent necessary vocabulary for communication in English? Can there be more than one basic word list? Is the basic word list simply a matter of identification of words that have a high frequency of use? What does it mean not to be in possession of a knowledge of vocabulary in the basic word list?

In a study by Kersey (1970), the Dolch Common Noun List and the Dolch 220 Word List were compared to a word list from a population of Seminole Indian children. The children's words came from stories used by third and fourth graders. The Seminole word list contained 67.7 percent of the words on the Dolch 220 Word List. But it also contained 149 service words that were not on the list. The Seminole word list contained 63.2 percent of the words on the Dolch Common Noun List plus 189 nouns that were not on the Dolch list. How is the educator to explain this? Is one list better than another? Is a child smarter if he or she knows one or the other list? In short, the meaning of "basic word list" is ambiguous, with fatal results for standardized testing. To treat a single basic word list as universally valid is absurd.

Let's examine the concept of "word difficulty." Is a word difficult because only a few people know it? Is a word easy because many people know it? On many standardized test items, difficulty is determined by statistical methods. Yet it is not clear just what the nature of the difficulty is. The assumptions about difficulty are not explicated. Therefore, what is being tested, difficulty or familiarity?

What about "vocabulary"? Notice the word "vocabulary" is unqualified. Is it a Chicago vocabulary, a Bronx vocabulary, a Boston vocabulary, a Tennessee vocabulary? Is there a universal American vocabulary? If not, do we measure a person's vocabulary, or do we simply try to determine if a person has learned a particular vocabulary? Are we measuring vocabulary ability—the ability to learn words? What is the linguistic rationale for expecting all Americans to have identical vocabularies? What are the criteria for item selection for a vocabulary test? What is a vocabulary test?

I could go on with a similar treatment of "general information," "beginning and ending sounds," and "comprehension." However, the point should be clear: the constructs are ambiguous and the specifications of items are arbitrary! Therefore, the mass production of standardized tests and assessment procedures to measure the behaviors implied by the constructs is in reality the production of mass confusion.

In general, we are faced with a rampant, unbridled ethnocentricism among the designers of standardized tests and assessment procedures for use with populations of diverse cultural groups (Hilliard 1995). If tests are designed only as achievement measures, are content valid, and if the content is agreed to by clients, then there is little to concern us. It is only when the detection of pathology is implied that we must call for superior accountability in testing. The cure for this ethnocentric malady must address the ethnocentrism more than the study and analysis of African American children. William Labov's classic article, "The Logic of Non-Standard English" (1970), is an excellent piece of work in which he proves that "nonstandard English," meaning "African American language," has a logic. He didn't need to prove it to those who speak it. They have not changed. His work teaches the scholars who apparently have had a difficult time understanding African American speech.

Urgent Needs

It should be clear by now that Band-Aids will not do. It will take more than lay knowledge to respond to the fundamental issues. That means that cultural linguists who are familiar with linguistics and with the language of African Americans must be a part of an in-depth evaluation of how language is used in assessment and in the instructional process to see if it is scientifically appropriate. This principle applies to professional practices with any ethnic group. We have major changes to make in the whole system of education. Some of them are as follows.

There is an urgent need for systematic cultural-linguistic review of all testing and assessment devices that are used with African Americans. No existing instruments have been subjected to such a review by professionals who are competent in African American cultural linguistics. There is an urgent need to provide full and competent descriptions of the language that is spoken by African Americans. This language must be described in its historical and cultural context, and not as a simple contrast to common American English.

There is little need to teach teachers specific techniques for teaching the African American child. Teachers must be taught so that their total orientation toward language and cultural linguistic principles represents the best that we now know about the subject. It is not the bag of tricks but the general attitude of a teacher that is important. If an African American child is seen as language deficient, we can show that the behavior of the teacher actually changes toward that child as compared to "normal" children. He or she will engage the child in communication less and pay less attention to the child (e.g., see Aaron and Powell 1982; Irvine 1991; Simpson and Erickson 1983). *It is this teaching behavior and not the language of the child, no matter how different, that creates the problem for learners* (Johnson and Clement 1973; Nimnick and Johnson 1973).

It is one thing to say that the language context of African Americans must be taken into account in the teaching/learning process. It is quite another to know what to do about it. Both linguists and successful teachers and school leaders—those who are successful with African American children—must be provided with the time to develop and articulate their theories of positive and empowering pedagogy. (One example is the work of Ladson-Billings 1994.) We need no "Black language kits." The child's language presents no pedagogical problems. Cultural-linguistics review can show that this is true.

If chimpanzees (Warshoe at the Yerkes Primate Laboratory) can be taught to do American Sign Language, and if a chimpanzee can teach another chimpanzee to sign, and if a gorilla (Koko at Stanford) can earn a 90 on a human I.Q. test, then one would think that any human being could be taught the simple task of reading. All humans are capable of so much more.

Septima Clark is the creator of "freedom schools" in eleven Southern states. These schools were responsible for teaching reading to 12 million potential voters who were illiterate. In a short period of time (Clark seems to suggest about two or three years), the number of illiterates was reduced from 12 million to about 12,000, radically altering voting patterns in the South. I asked Septima Clark how she was able to accomplish such a feat. She responded, "I generally avoided using regular trained teachers." As a teacher educator, I was stunned. "Why would you do that?" I asked. She answered that often people who saw themselves as highly educated projected the idea to her students that they regarded themselves as better than the students. "Their education got in the way." Surely, there is a lesson in this for us, as we ponder the nature of our interventions to come.

Conclusion

Who teaches error in linguistic understanding? How do they do it? It is done in many subtle ways in everything from linguistic departments, to English classes, to teacher behavior, and to the mass media. We are faced with nothing less than the need to re-educate our nation to the truth about language. The public in general is not equipped to understand the language issues. We have a major communication problem, especially since so few professionals understand language issues either. There is no quick fix. It is important to conceptualize the problem in its broadest scope. We need no more analyses of the African American child. We need to renovate the system that teaches error. We have the tools to do the job. Do we have the will?

REFERENCES

Aaron, R., and G. Powell (1982). Feedback practices as a function of teacher pupil race during reading groups instruction. *Journal of Negro Education* 51; 50–59.

Alleyne, M. C. (1971). Linguistic continuity of Africa in the Caribbean. In H. J. Richards (ed.), *Topics in Afro-American Studies*; 118–34. New York: Black Academy Press.

Anderson, J. D. (1988). *The history of black education in the South: 1860–1935*. Chapel Hill: The University of North Carolina Press.

Carter, R. T., and A. L. Goodwin (1994). Racial identity and education. In L. Darling-Hammond (ed.), *Review of Research in Education*, vol. 20, 291–336. Washington, D.C.: American Educational Research Association.

Chase, A. (1977). *The legacy of Malthus*. New York: Knopf.

Cohen, R. (1969). Conceptual styles, culture conflict, and non-verbal tests of intelligence. *American Anthropologist* 71(5); 828–57.

College Board (1985). *Equity and excellence: The educational status of Black Americans*. New York: Author.

D'Andrade, R. (1995). *The development of cognitive anthropology*. New York: Cambridge University Press.

Fromkin, V., and R. Rodman (1993). *An introduction to language*. New York: Holt, Rinehart and Winston.

Goodlad, J. I. (1984). *A place called school*. New York: McGraw Hill.

Guthrie, R. (1976). *Even the rat was white*. New York: Harper and Row.

Hegel, G.W.F. (1831). *The philosophy of history* (J. Sibree, trans.). Buffalo, NY: Prometheus.

Hilliard, A. G., III. (1983). Psychological factors associated with language in education of the African American child. *Journal of Negro Education* 52(1); 24–34.

——— (1990). Misunderstanding and testing intelligence. In J. I. Goodlad and P. Keating (eds.), *Access to knowledge*, 145–58. New York: College Board.

————(ed.) (1995). *Testing African American Students*. Chicago: Third World Press.

———— (1996). Either a paradigm shift or no mental measurement: The non-science and nonsense of *The Bell Curve*. *Cultural Diversity and Mental Health Journal* 2(1); 1–20.

Hoover, M. R., R. L. Politzer, and O. Taylor (1995). Bias in reading tests for black language speakers: A sociolinguistic perspective. In Hilliard, Asa G. III (ed.), *Testing African American students*, 51–68. Chicago: Third World Press.

Irvine, J. J. (1991). *Black students and school failure*. New York: Praeger.

Johnson, J. A., and D. C. Clement (1973). *Incongruences between experience bases of lower income urban black children and experiences requisite to success in schools*. In G. P. Nimnick and J. A. Johnson (eds.), *Beyond compensatory education: A new approach to educating children*, 95–109. San Francisco: Far West Laboratory for Educational Research and Development.

Kamin, L. (1974). *The science and politics of I.Q.* New York: Wiley.

Kersey, H. A., Jr. (1970). The Federal day school as the acculturation agent for Seminole Indian children. Paper presented at the annual meeting of the American Education Research Association, Minneapolis. April (ERIC No. ED 039 988).

King, J. (1971). *Pan Africanism and education: A study of race, philanthropy and education in the southern states of America and East Africa*. Oxford: Clarendon Press.

Labov, W. (1970). The logic of non-standard English. In F. Williams (ed.), *Language and Poverty*, 153–89. Chicago: Markham.

Ladson-Billings, G. (1994). *The dreamkeepers: successful teachers of African American children*. San Francisco: Jossey-Bass.

Nimnick, G. P., and J. A. Johnson (1973). *Beyond compensatory education: A new approach to educating children*. San Francisco: Far West Laboratory for Educational Research and Development.

Oakes, J., and M. Lipton (1990). Tracking and ability grouping: A structural barrier to access and achievement. In J. I. Goodlad and P. Keating (eds.), *Access to knowledge*, 187–204. New York: College Board.

Rowe, H. A. H. (ed.) (1991). *Intelligence, reconceptualization and measurement.* Australian Council for Educational Research. Hillsdale, NJ: Lawrence Erlbaum.

Salomon, G. (1995). Reflections on the field of educational psychology by outgoing journal editor. *Educational Psychologist* 30(3); 105–08.

Shuy, R. W. (1977). Quantitative linguistic analysis: A case for and some warnings against. *Anthropology and Education Quarterly* 1(2); 78–82.

Simpson, A. W., and M. T. Erickson (1983). Teachers' verbal and non-verbal communication patterns as a function of teacher race, student gender, and student race. *American Educational Research Journal* 20; 269–88.

Smith, E. (1978). The retention of phonological, phonemic, and morphophonemic features of Africa in Afro-American ebonics. Seminar Paper 43. Fullerton, CA: Department of Linguistics, California State University, Fullerton.

Snyderman, M., and S. Rothman (1990). *The IQ controversy: The media and public policy.* New Brunswick, NJ: Transaction.

Spivey, D. (1978). *Schooling for the new slavery: Black industrial education, 1868–1915.* Westport, CT: Greenwood.

Turner, L. (1969). *Africanism in the Gullah dialect.* New York: Arno.

Vass, W. K. (1974). *The Bantu speaking heritage of the United States.* Los Angeles: Center for Afro-American Studies, University of California.

CHAPTER 7

I ain't
writin' nuttin':
Permissions to Fail
and Demands to
Succeed in
Urban Classrooms

GLORIA J. LADSON-BILLINGS

GLORIA LADSON-BILLINGS raises an enormous red flag, and raises it high. In a first-grade classroom, a child is about to be educationally shortchanged. Shannon, a six-year-old speaker of African American language, has been asked to think of a sentence about something special, share that sentence, and then write it down. It's a clear assignment. However, all that it takes for Shannon to be passed over with a "maybe you'll feel like writing tomorrow" from her teacher is a shake of the little girl's head and a firm announcement, "I ain't writin' nuttin'!" In contrast, Ladson-Billings tells us about a teacher who galvanizes his poor and working-class African American students who "hate" to write by creating culturally responsive lessons that include music and drama as precursors to writing. Their final written piece is fueled by their creativity and carefully crafted—the result of much discussion and numerous edits. It is fine, the author tells us, to empathize with your students, but don't allow their language or attitudes to lower expectations of their abilities or to compromise your own willingness to seek creative educational solutions.

Picture a classroom of kindergarten and first grade students. The class has about thirty students with two certificated teachers. Despite the lower teacher-student ratio, the number of children in a relatively small classroom makes it a rather crowded place. Monday morning often starts with the teachers initiating a sharing activity. Each of the students is asked to think of a sentence that describes something special that happened to him or her over the weekend. All of the students will have an opportunity to share their sentences with the other students at their tables. Ultimately, the students will choose one sentence and attempt to write it.

On this particular morning, Shannon*, an African American girl, is sitting at her table with Audrey, Denny, and Keith, three White children. The two White boys immediately begin sharing sentences. Denny's sentence is "I went to my grandma's anniversary party and I played outside." The three White students agree that Denny has proposed a good sentence—one with eleven words! After a moment the students notice that Shannon has not contributed. "What did you do last weekend, Shannon?" asks Audrey. "Oh, nuttin'," replies Shannon. Denny and Keith agree that the table should choose Denny's sentence to write. Shannon remarks to Keith, "You always choose his sentences!" Keith says, "We don't pick your sentences 'cause you're too grumpy!" Shannon snaps

*All classroom participants in this study are given pseudonyms.

back, "I don't want no White people pickin' me!" There is an eerie silence and then the other children settle down to begin writing. Shannon only writes the word, "I" and begins to complain that she cannot write the word, "grandma."

After a few minutes one of the teachers comes by this table and notices that Shannon is just sitting while the others are working at constructing the sentence. "Would you like to try writing your sentence today, Shannon?" Shannon shakes her head no, arises from the table and begins to wander around the room. The teacher says to her as she begins wandering, "That's okay. Maybe you'll feel like writing tomorrow." This is not an isolated incident. On a previous visit my coinvestigator witnessed Shannon talking with Audrey. Audrey asked Shannon what she was writing. Shannon snapped, "I ain't writin' nuttin'!"

What both my coinvestigator and I saw was what I term "permission to fail." Although most students were encouraged to write each day, Shannon was regularly permitted to fail. Her refusal to write was not just stubbornness but a ploy to cover up her inability to read, or more specifically, her lack of phonemic awareness. Witnessing this pattern of avoidance is difficult for me as an African American female parent and researcher. Are there teachers permitting my daughter to fail? Are there teachers in classrooms across the country permitting children to fail? I cannot help but wonder if the permission to fail was granted Shannon so easily, in part, because her cultural style, form of language, and attitude deemed her unworthy of teaching in her teachers' eyes.

My own scholarly work has been grounded in what I have termed "culturally relevant pedagogy." I have written about it in a variety of other places (see for example, Ladson-Billings, 1994; 1995). It is a theoretical construct that rests on three propositions:

Successful teaching focuses on students' academic achievement,

Successful teaching supports students' cultural competence, and

Successful teaching promotes students' socio-political consciousness.

Students' academic achievement represents intellectual growth
and the ability to produce knowledge. Regardless of whatever else
schools do, students are supposed to learn something. That learning
can be manifested in student competency in a variety of subject
areas and skills. Can students read, write, problem-solve, make critical decisions? Each of these can represent examples of students'
academic achievement.

Cultural competence refers to the ability of students to grow in
understanding and respect for their culture of origin. Rather than
experiencing the alienating effects of education where school-based
learning detaches students from their home culture, cultural competence is a way for students to be bicultural and facile in the
ability to move between school and home cultures.

Socio-political consciousness is an attempt to help students develop a sense of mutuality and reciprocity toward others with
whom they share cultural solidarity. It is designed to help students
ask larger socio-political questions about how schools and the society work to expose ongoing inequity and social injustice. If students do not begin to ask these questions, they are likely to
reiterate positions that suggest that the reason people are unsuc-
cessful in school is that they do not try hard enough. Culturally
relevant teaching is designed to help students move past a blaming
the victim mentality and search for the structural and symbolic
foundations of inequity and injustice.

Demanding Success

For three years I worked with a group of eight elementary teachers
working in predominantly African American school classrooms who
did not grant children permission to fail. Instead they demanded
that they succeed. What does a classroom that demands success

from all students look like? What opportunities and requirements for success do they present?

Over the last five or six years I have written and spoken often of my work with successful teachers of African American students (Ladson-Billings, 1994). In some circles I think the stories of those teachers have grown "larger than life." Once a school district official called to invite me to speak to the district's teachers. "Oh, and can you bring those eight teachers with you?" she asked. Somehow, these women who do serious and important work with African American students had become something of a "road show." This sense of entertainment that I may have conveyed in my writing trivializes the day-to-day hard work of teaching that happens in their classrooms. It mystifies them. But what they do is not mystical or magical. It is well thought out, careful, reflective practice undergirded by a commitment to the students' academic achievement, their cultural competence, and their socio-political consciousness.

In an attempt to move past the perceived "magic" of the dream-keepers I have begun to look carefully at the practice of novice teachers. I have selected novices because of my desire to understand how people learn to be good teachers and by extension how we (teacher educators) teach them to be good teachers. Currently, I am analyzing data from a data set of eight novice teachers. It would be premature for me to draw conclusions given the current messiness of the data. However, I can share some things I learned from another novice teacher that pointed me in the direction of novice teachers as a possible site for excellence in urban classrooms.

Carter Forshay was excited about his first teaching job. He had completed his undergraduate degree at a midwestern university not far from his hometown. After undergraduate school he made his way to the West Coast, an area of the country he longed to see. While there he completed a teacher certification program and accepted a job offer from a large urban school district in California. As a young, twenty-something African American male, this job in an exciting, vibrant city seemed a perfect opportunity. Carter began his first year with the youthful enthusiasm, energy and idealism of the uninitiated. He made a commitment to ensure that his fourth graders would demonstrate high levels of literacy. His undergraduate degree was in communications and in the back of his mind he harbored thoughts of completing a masters degree in the field that might lead to a career in communications. In the meantime, Carter saw teaching as a socially responsible, positive career even if it was not financially lucrative.

Carter's first jolt back to reality came when he learned that his students absolutely hated writing. Several of them were respectable readers, given that the expectations for African American poor and working-class students are exceedingly low. But almost none of the children enjoyed writing. Each time Carter attempted to come up with an exciting and motivating topic on which to write, his students balked. "Ah, Mr. Forshay, I don't want to do this." "Writin' is too hard." "I don't have nothin' to say, why are you makin' us write stuff?" "Why can't you just give us some worksheets? We can do them!" Each day these comments and similar ones greeted Carter whenever he proposed a writing task. After several half-hearted attempts on the part of the students and mounting frustration on the part of the teacher, Carter began a systematic examination of his own practice. This is a significant step because he clearly could have chosen another course of action. Carter began to think about what kinds of things were important in his life. Chief among them was music. Carter had an extensive collection of vintage and contemporary jazz. He knew his students also loved music although their musical taste ran more toward rap and soul. Carter decided to gamble that if he could help the kids connect with music, he could help them connect with writing. Carter chose a CD by trumpeter Wynton Marsalis that featured a song entitled, "Blue Interlude: The Bittersweet Saga of Sugar Cane and Sweetie Pie." He chose this song because on it Marsalis explains the way he uses the various melodies to reflect particular "characters." During the first lesson Carter played the CD and led the students in a discussion of what they thought the action was and how they thought the characters were feeling and behaving. From there Carter encouraged the students to take turns role-playing the characters and their interactions. Once one of the girls took the role of Sweetie Pie and two boys became Sugar Cane and Cotton Candy, the rest of the students delighted in the action. Some students would urge Sweetie Pie to play hard to get. Others would tell Sugar Cane he had to be cooler. Students took turns acting out these roles, each threesome more dramatic and emotive than the preceding one. From their dramatic interpretations Carter helped small groups of students develop character webs for each of the main characters.

On the next day Carter replayed the CD and asked students to review their character webs. Were there any changes they wanted to make? Did their webs best reflect what they believed about the characters? After some changes to the character webs Carter encouraged the students to talk about the kind of story the characters might be involved in. Next, the students began to write some dialogue for their stories. Each group of students shared the dialogues with every other group. The groups made suggestions for change and the students began a rough draft of the story. Carter had the students compare their rough drafts with the premises on which their stories were based. They ended the second day's lesson with thinking about what needed to be added or deleted from their stories.

On the third day Carter had the students review their rough drafts. He asked each group to provide feedback to each of the other groups. The students used the feedback to revise and edit the rough drafts. They then completed illustrations for the finished work. The lesson closed with students publishing their books and sharing them with students from other classrooms. Below is the text of their story:

Sugar Cane's Dream
By Room 19
Based on Blue Interlude:
The Bittersweet Saga of Sugar Cane and Sweetie Pie
By the Wynton Marsalis Septet

One night a man named Sugar Cane went into a bar. There he met a lady named Sweetie Pie. Thus, began their blue interlude. Sugar Cane wanted a beer because he was thirsty. He walked into a bar and saw a beautiful woman working behind the bar. He went over to her and she said, "Hi, my name is Sweetie Pie. How are you doing?"

"Fine thanks," Sugar Cane said and then asked for a beer.

Sweetie Pie said, "Why not? A handsome man like you can have anything from my bar!" They talked for a while. They found out they had a lot in common. Finally, Sugar Cane said, "You look beautiful. Do you want to go out on a date?"

"Yes." Sweetie Pie said.

Sugar Cane said, "I'll pick you up at eight o'clock tomorrow night."

"Meet me here at the bar," Sugar Pie replied.

They decided to go to a restaurant. Sugar Cane asked for Sweetie Pie's phone number. They talked until Sweetie Pie got off from work. Sweetie Pie asked Sugar Cane if he had a car and when he said he didn't, she offered him a ride home which he accepted. On the way home, they continued their conversation. They talked about their jobs, sports, and what restaurant they were going to on their date.

"I'll see you tomorrow at eight," Sweetie Pie said when she dropped him off.

Sugar Cane couldn't stop thinking about Sweetie Pie. He remembered he had her phone number so he called her at home. Sugar Cane told Sweetie Pie over the phone that they were going to the Crystal Light Restaurant on 33rd Street.

The next morning Sugar Cane called Sweetie Pie to check if their date was still it. She said it was. Sugar Cane was nervous about the date. It took him three hours to get dressed. He put on a suit and tie. The suit was black and the tie was white. Sweetie Pie took one hour to get dressed. She wore a red dress with a white collar, red choker, and red high heels.

When Sugar Cane got to the bar he saw Sweetie Pie with another man. In shock, he walked over to them and demanded that she tell him who he was.

Sweetie Pie said, "This is my boyfriend from college. His name is Cotton Candy. He called me last night and told me he was in town. He wanted to go out."

Cotton Candy said politely to Sugar Cane, "Do you want to join us?"

"No," Sugar Cane yelled. "I spent three hours getting ready. I put on nice cologne and here you are with another man! How could you do this to me?"

"She's my girlfriend!" exclaimed Cotton Candy.

Sweetie Pie broke in, "First of all I had a date with Sugar Cane, also I had a date with you, Cotton Candy."

"Sweetie Pie that don't explain nothin'," Sugar Cane said.

Sweetie Pie rolled her eyes and said, "Oh well."

Sugar Cane cried, "Just what I thought! I've had enough of this. I'm going to get myself a drink. I knew something was going to go wrong." He then went off to get his drink.

Cotton Candy said, "You have another boyfriend?"

Sweetie Pie said, "Yes, you have a problem with that? You can't say nothin' cause you called out of nowhere."

"You didn't tell me you had another boyfriend." Cotton Candy walked away from Sweetie Pie and left the bar.

Sweetie Pie walked over to the bar to talk with Sugar Cane. Sweetie Pie told Sugar Cane, "I'm sorry for what I did to you. I got carried away. I apologize."

"I accept your apology but I can't go out with you. What you did was unacceptable and I hope you don't do it to another man," Sugar Cane said.

They went their separate ways.

Two weeks later Sweetie Pie called Sugar Cane. She apologized for dissin' him.

"I'm sorry for dissin' you. I was out of control. Can we try again?"

Sugar Cane answered, "I guess so under one condition—
that you don't diss me again."

The End

Carter's dogged determination that his students acquire appropriate literacy skills required that he recognize the language and
literacy skills the students already possessed and connect them up
with conventional forms of literacy.

Carter's push for literacy represents a demand for success. He
could have given in to the students' complaints and compromised
with worksheets. He could have pushed for writing the way he
began even when the students were reluctant and producing very
poor quality writing. But both of those choices would have repre-
sented permission to fail. They would have conveyed to students
that it was perfectly all right for them to stay where they were
because no one, especially their teacher, expected very much of
them. Instead, Carter decided to demand success.

Carter took responsibility for moving the students from what James
Gee (1998) argues is reading and writing with a small "r" and
small "w" to reading and writing with a big "R" and big "W."
According to Gee, small "r" reading and small "w" writing refer
to "learning, knowledge, performance, or interaction where the
focus is on the design features of written language" (p. 5). On the
other hand, Big "R" reading and Big "W" writing refer to "any
specific social practice or activity in which reading and writing are
involved together with distinctive meanings, values, attitudes, ways
of acting, interacting using oral language and other symbol systems
that these practices or activities recruit or require," *in other words,
using reading and writing for real purposes* [italics added]. A failure
to understand this distinction between small and big r and w reading and writing is what keeps us locked in warring camps we
sometimes call "whole language" versus "phonics," "literature-
based" versus "skill-based." There is the temptation to read Carter

as an African American male with an automatic "in" with the students he was teaching. However, that would be a serious misreading. Carter was from a middle-class family. His mother was a teacher. His dad was an engineer. He was a graduate of an elite private university. Carter's students came from the poorest section of the city. To them Carter was something of a nerd. He didn't wear cool clothes and he didn't talk like the guys in their neighborhood. Although he was a young man, he seemed more like somebody's father than an older brother. But Carter wasn't a father. He also wasn't a veteran teacher and colleagues expected him to follow their lead. They taught with worksheets. They accepted mediocrity. They permitted students to fail. But Carter held some basic beliefs about the students that supported his pedagogy and made their academic success more likely. Carter believed that the students had the capacity to learn whatever he taught them. His major obstacle was not the students' ability, it was pedagogical limitation. To meet the academic goals he had set, Carter had to rethink his practice in some fundamental ways. He had to keep asking himself as Haberman (1995) suggests, "I wonder what I do next?" He had to keep a sense of uncertainty and a willingness to question in the forefront of his teaching. Carter believed that it was important to protect learners and learning (Haberman, 1995). More specifically, while Carter empathized with the students' struggle to write he understood that his job was to teach them to do it. He didn't put them down for not enjoying writing or writing well, but he also did not let them off the hook. He had to help them appreciate the power and fulfillment of writing and he had to preserve each student's sense of self.

Carter believed that it was important to put ideas into practice. While I have come to know many teachers (many of them eager young preservice teachers) who can "talk a good game" when it comes to teaching, I know a much smaller subset of teachers who can actually turn that talk into meaningful and productive academic experiences for students. Carter not only had an idea for stimulating the students' interest in writing, he developed a series of pedagogical actions that he needed to take to make that idea a reality. Today's teacher is not without ideas for teaching. The journals, teaching magazines, workshops, institutes, and conferences all provide resources for "what" to teach. The major stumbling block is how to make use of those resources in local, specific classroom contexts.

Carter believed it was important to cultivate a professional-personal stance with his students. Each day Carter Forshay came to school wearing a freshly starched shirt, oftentimes a tie, sometimes a jacket, other times a sweater. He wore slacks or suit trousers, never jeans. This "professional" attire may seem superficial and tangential to the task, but Carter realized that as a young Black man it was easy for him to be mistaken for something other than a teacher. As a young African American man he felt an obligation to present an image of African American maleness beyond that of the hip-hop rapper or gang banger. This carefully cultivated image is equally important for his students and his colleagues. In the classroom Carter could not be described as demonstrative or as a "warm fuzzy" teacher. He has a business-like demeanor. Carter does not talk about "loving" his students. Rather he focuses on "caring" about and for them. This care is manifested in Carter's insistence on high levels of academic achievement for all students.

Teachers like Carter Forshay give me some hope that we can prepare teachers who will demand success from all students. They reinforce my belief that there is no magic in technique, curriculum, or strategy. The "magic" is in the teaching.

Epilogue—Ethical Considerations

As I close I must return to a point that continues to plague me in my work. At the beginning of this paper I talked about the little African American girl Shannon's refusal to write and her teachers' permitting her to evade the daily assignments while simultaneously allowing her to slip further and further behind her classmates. Shannon's first steps on the road to failure are not likely to lead her to a satisfactory ending.

Shannon is being allowed to fail. No demands are being made for her to perform at the same levels as her peers. Her resistance is a challenge for her teachers but it is their challenge. At six years old Shannon must not be allowed to determine her own demise. She is dependent upon caring adults to act in responsible ways. Just as we would not allow Shannon to stick her fingers in a roaring flame or ride in our cars without being carefully buckled with a seat belt, we must recognize the impending danger of her proclamation, "I ain't writin' nuttin'!"

REFERENCES

Gee, J. P. (1998). Preamble to a literacy program. Unpublished document. University of Wisconsin, Madison (March).

Haberman, M. (1995). Star teachers of children in poverty. Bloomington, IN: Kappa Delta Pi.

Kelley, R.D.G. (1998). Yo' mama is disfunktional! Fighting the culture wars in urban America. Boston: Beacon Press.

Ladson-Billings, G. (1994). The dreamkeepers: successful teachers of African American children. San Francisco: Jossey Bass.

———— (1995). Toward a theory of culturally relevant pedagogy. American Educational Research Journal, 35, 465–491.

CHAPTER 8

"...As Soon As She Opened Her Mouth!": Issues of Language, Literacy, and Power

VICTORIA PURCELL-GATES

Language discrimination is not always a Black-White issue. VICTORIA PURCELL-GATES's two-year ethnography of a White family from southern Appalachia introduces us to Donny, the barely literate young boy of two barely literate parents. Donny was written off as a hopeless case by his teachers as early as second grade. He had not ever been exposed to the acts of reading and writing before coming to school, and had not, therefore, developed a concept of literacy as many of his middle-class peers had. His teachers treated this difference in experience as an intellectual deficiency: instead of introducing Donny to the culture of literacy and helping him use his oral language to access the printed word, they assumed that he was less capable of learning and associated his hillbilly language with intractable ignorance. It is the duty of teachers to guide all students to literacy with equal rigor, insists Purcell-Gates, without ever telling them that the language they speak is wrong.

A warm afternoon in a midwestern U.S. city: A fourth-grade teacher grinned up at me knowingly as she condemned a young mother: "I knew she was ignorant just as soon as she opened her mouth!" This teacher was referring to the fact that Jenny, the mother of Donny, one of her students, spoke in a southern mountain dialect, a dialect that is often used to characterize poor whites known variously as "hillbillies," "hicks," or "ridgerunners." As this teacher demonstrated, this dialect is strongly associated with low levels of education and literacy as well as a number of social ills and dysfunctions. And sure enough, Donny, the child of parents who could neither read nor write anything except for their names, was failing to become literate in school as well.

A warm afternoon in a rural village in El Salvador: A 66-year-old Salvadoran campesina (peasant), Maria Jesus, explained to my co-researcher why, when she was young, children in her village did not go to school: "All five student that were there [school] didn't learn anything. So there was no reason to go. And it was too far from where we lived. It was really far; we had to cross the trails, and there was a ravine that got so full in the winter, we couldn't get through."

Researchers around the world have been focused on this problem: the cavernous and uncrossable ravine that seems to lie between children of poverty (and the adults they grow up to be) from marginalized, or low-status, groups and their full potentials as literate beings. Overall, the best we have been able to do is to describe the situation over and over again, using different measures, different definitions of literacy, different theoretical lenses, different methodologies. Again and again we conclude that in developed countries and in third-world countries, learners from impoverished and low-status groups fail to develop as fully and productively literate as compared to learners from sociocultural groups that hold sociopolitical power and favor. Further, this reality continues despite what appears to be clear identification of the problem, and billions of dollars spent by national governments and international agencies. It is this relationship between class and power, language and literacy that I write about here. I have pursued this topic in a number of research projects, and I'll draw a few examples from these.

Some children bring "literacy knowledge" to school with them. Does this mean that they already knew how to read? How to write? No, such literacy knowledge refers to the concepts children acquire during their preschool years, during the years preceding the beginning of formal literacy instruction, in kindergarten and first grade, in reading, writing and printed language.

Let me give you some examples: A little girl about two years old was sitting with her mother in the parents/children room at church one Sunday. Bored with the actual church service, this little girl asked her mother to read to her. Her mother, trying to focus on the service, put her off for as long as she could. "Read!" commanded the child, "read!" Her mother, silently following along in her Bible, said, "I AM reading." "No!" said the two-year-old. Reaching up with her hand, she opened her mother's mouth and began to move her lips up and down.

Another example: A four-year-old boy was experimenting with paper and pencil one day during a quiet time at home. Suddenly he rushed up to his mother, holding out a piece of paper with some scribbles on it. "Mommy!" he cried. "What did I write?" "What did I write?" "I don't know sweetie. What did you write?" answered his mother. "I don't know! I can't read!" he cried.

Both of these children have acquired some basic, crucial, concepts about reading and about written language. And they learned these concepts not by being formally taught, but by being there and part of the action when important people in their lives were reading and writing for their own purposes. The little girl had figured out that "reading" meant that activity which happened when her mother would read aloud to her, something that inevitably meant her mouth was open and her lips moving. Silent reading was not known to this child yet, since she had not observed it (or did not know that she had). The little boy also knew some important things about reading/writing and written language. He knew that people wrote by making marks on a piece of paper. He also knew that one could read what someone had written. Through experimentation, he realized that he had "written" something. He also knew enough at this point to know that while he may have written something, he did not know how to read it!

These examples probably seem very familiar to all of you who have had young children. In fact, young children behaving in this way, and doing things like pointing to an exit sign in a store and asking "What does that say?" or writing the first letter of their names in crayon on the living room wall, seem part of the natural way of children. All children do these things, don't they?

In fact, all children do not behave in ways that let us know that they have learned and are learning about written language when they are very young. That is because not all children learn about written language to the same extent during their pre-formal instruction years. To learn about written language, to learn that "print says." To learn that written stories sound different from the way people talk, to learn that letters make words and words make sentences, and that when you read you must begin at the left and move your eyes across to the right and then go back to the left again, to learn that letters stand for individual sounds—to learn all of these basic concepts requires extensive experience with people using print, with people reading and writing around you and to you and for you and allowing you to try your hand at reading and writing.

The degree to which you do not experience these extensive uses of print in your young life is the degree to which you do not know/ understand the concepts that are so crucial to making sense out of beginning reading and writing instruction in school.

Social Class and Emergent Literacy Knowledge

To explore this relationship between experience with print and emergent literacy knowledge and a possible link to social class membership, I conducted, along with Karin Dahl, a two-year study of kindergarten and first-grade children (Purcell-Gates & Dahl, 1991). We began by measuring the emergent literacy knowledge held by these children from economically stressed homes. We found that, across the board, these children had less knowledge of written language and how reading and writing work than children from more middle-class homes.

We then followed them through their first two years of school, documenting their literacy instruction and the ways in which they made sense of it. We found that by the end of first grade, those children who began kindergarten with more knowledge of written language, and especially more knowledge of the functions of print in the real world—what we called The Big Picture—were the most active learners and the most successful readers at the end of first grade.

What does this suggest? It suggests, among other things, that children who *experience* other people in their lives reading and writing for many different reasons in the years before they begin school are better equipped conceptually to make sense of—to learn from—the beginning reading and writing instruction in their schools. It also suggests that, as a group, children from homes of poverty experience fewer instances of people reading and writing for a broad number of purposes than do children from mainstream homes. To the extent that parental education—which is going to affect the frequency and the types of reading and writing people do—is related to poverty, this makes some sense.

I followed up on this two-year study with, first, a single case study (Purcell-Gates, 1995) and then a larger study of twenty families with young children from low-income homes to document how much people read and wrote in these homes and what kinds of things they read and wrote (Purcell-Gates, 1996). Looking at the larger study first, I documented that, yes, overall there were relatively few instances of reading and writing in these homes; but there was a range from almost no uses of print to print use that looked just like the middle-class homes described by others (Taylor, 1985). Further, by measuring the emergent literacy knowledge of the young children in the homes, I found clear relationships between both frequency of reading and writing events in the homes and children's conceptual knowledge of written language and between the kinds of reading and writing events and children's emergent literacy knowledge. The more parents read and wrote beyond simple clauses like you find on cereal boxes and coupons, and the more they involved their young children in reading and writing events: pointing out letters, sounds, words, and reading to their children, or involving their children in reading events that focused on things of interest to the children, the more those children knew The Big Picture. They knew different concepts of print, the alphabetic nature of our print system, and that letters stand for sounds.

Conversely, looking at the case study of Donny and his mother, Jenny, the parent and child with which I began this paper, I documented the degree to which the almost total lack of reading and writing events in the home can present a serious challenge to young children's ability to learn from school instruction on reading and writing. In Donny's home, because neither parent could read nor write, the children grew up understanding that life did not include print. In fact, they did not understand that print existed as a meaningful semiotic system; it did not "mean," did not function in their lives. And they lived full and interesting lives without it. This was, I believe, a key insight I came to as I worked with and collected data from this family over two years. Donny, the little school-aged boy of the family, did not, could not, make sense of the beginning literacy instruction he received in school. Without an understanding that written language *communicates*—that it *means*, he had no idea what to do when he was "taught" to "sound out" words, to match beginning letter sounds, to fill in blanks using words he was supposed to have learned.

Language, Literacy, and Power

At this point I want to stop and caution you about where you may think I am going with this. It is true that I have been busy documenting knowledge—specifically, knowledge of written language—that children from homes of poverty lack, or hold to lesser degrees, than children from more middle-class homes. I have also been documenting the degree to which this knowledge and lack of it affects their ability to learn to read and write in school. However, I want to state *unequivocally* that this is not a deficit theory, nor is it placing the blame on the children, their parents, or their homes. This is where the "Power" part of my title comes in.

What I have been describing, and what I have been documenting, is *experience*, I have been documenting the ways in which experience—in this case, experience with written language use—varies across homes. What I am saying is that children come to school with different experiences. The experiences they have as young children are culturally driven. Within this, I see literacy use as cultural practice. It is cultural practice because reading and writing are woven into the everyday experiences of people, and these everyday activities, attitudes, and beliefs help to define and distinguish among cultural groups.

The implications of this stance of cultural *difference* instead of *deficit* for educators is profound. Let me try to make this point with an illustration—an example—of cultural difference that could affect education. Let's imagine an educational situation in which experience is significant but not as politically charged as that of literacy. Let's think about driver's education, for example. Let's say that a young man enrolls in a driver's education course along with twenty other young people. However, this young man has just arrived from the desert of Palestine or from a rural village in Afghanistan. The other twenty enrollees are from either the United States or another western country where almost everyone drives and rides in automobiles. Let's also assume that this young immigrant speaks, reads, and writes English. The driver's ed instructor comes to understand that this man, Phil, does not have a clue about cars. He does not understand how they run, the purposes for which they are used, the ways in which drivers drive, steer, brake, push the gas pedal, or stay on the right side of the road. All of the written materials, the drivers manuals, the ways in which the instructor instructs the class, depend on this background knowledge, this previous experience with car use. For example, "Put your key in the ignition, and turn it to start the car." Phil thinks, "Key"? "Ignition"? "Start"?

Are we going to interpret this as a flaw, a deficit, in Phil? Or are we going to interpret it as a lack of crucial experience, a difference in the experiential backgrounds between Phil and the other members of the drivers education class?

It does make a difference how we interpret this. If we assume that Phil's problem is due to a deficit, it is easier to write him off, tell him he cannot learn to drive, or put him in a remedial drivers ed class that gives the same classroom instruction at a slower pace, but still without giving him experience with cars. However, if we assume—rightly, I believe—that Phil's difficulties stem from a lack of actual experience with cars, and recognize the importance and role of that experience in learning to drive, we can set about providing that experience with cars that Phil—through no inherent fault of his own, or of the culture in which he grew up—has not had up to this point. We can give Phil lots of experiences with riding in cars, with observing other people driving cars, with exploring cars and how they work, with observing how important cars are to this culture in which he now lives.

Can we look at differences among children in the amount and type of written language experiences they have had before schooling in the same way, without assigning inherent deficit, or inability to learn, to children who do not have as much literary knowledge as other children? I believe so; I believe that if we claim to allow equal access to educational opportunity to all children in our schools then we must. But I also know that whether we interpret differences among children—or adults—as *deficit* or *difference* depends primarily on our preconceptions, attitudes toward, and stereotypes we hold toward the individual children's communities and cultures. If the child's family is poor, his parents undereducated, his dialect nonstandard, then we are much more likely to interpret experiential difference as a deficit in the child, in the parents, in the home, in the sociocultural community within which this child has grown up. And when we do this, we play God, conferring or denying educational opportunity to individual, socioculturally different, children. And we do not have the right to do this.

This was the second key insight I came to as a result of my two-year ethnography of Donny's family. While documenting the effect of growing up in a nonliterate family on Donny's conceptual knowledge of written language and the problems this posed for his learning to read and write in school, I had to ask what the school was doing about this. How were they dealing with this experiential difference so that his learning could proceed? Nothing. Absolutely nothing. Not only were they failing to address this experiential difference—much like our pretend driver's ed instructor would have addressed Phil's inexperience with cars—they were also seemingly unconcerned about his failure to learn.

How could this be? Having seen two of my own children through elementary schools and having garnered a wealth of experience with schools in general, I knew that teachers, specialists, and administrators would have created quite a big fuss if any middle-class child finished first grade knowing how to read only one word. Parents would be called and consulted, assuming they hadn't already been haunting the school corridors, testing would have been recommended and carried out, the instruction and teaching would have been questioned and examined, and elaborate educational plans drawn up to remediate this issue would have been drawn up.

But no notice was taken of Donny's failure to learn—except by his mother. Oh yes, Jenny knew that Donny wasn't learning. She recognized a very familiar and ominous pattern. Donny was not learning to read and write just as she and Donny's father had not learned to read and write. "I don't want what happened to us to happen to my son," she told me. "It's hard not knowing how to read! I know!" She worried that they would just pass him along until he eventually dropped out of school, just as she and her husband had both done in their seventh-grade years.

Jenny was down at her son's school constantly. She would go down to tell them that neither she nor his dad could read so please don't send notes home, but to call if they needed to talk to her. She would go down to try to tell them that Donny did not know enough about reading to be passed on to second grade. She would go down to complain that even though the teacher had told her that she would retain him in second grade, that he had been passed on to third—just as had happened to her and her husband.

As if she had never appeared before them, the teachers and the principal continued to send written notes home, never to call, and to complain officially that the parents never responded to messages.

As if she had never appeared before them, they passed Donny to second grade, dismissing her concerns about his failure to learn.

As if she had never appeared before them, they passed him on to third grade. They passed him on to third grade until, someone— a real person in their eyes—called to express concern and support for the idea that he be retained in second grade. You see, when Donny was passed on to third grade, I had been working with him and his family for a year. Jenny called to tell me what had happened. So I called the school office to request the right to attend a conference with the principal that Jenny believed she had arranged. As a result of this phone call, the school secretary took note of the fact that Dr. Purcell-Gates was also concerned about the failure of the school to retain Donny in second grade, as was promised by his second-grade teacher. An hour after this call, the secretary called me back and informed me that the principal would see to it that Donny was moved to a second-grade classroom if I believed that was best. An actual meeting with the principal of this school was never conducted.

Why wasn't Jenny listened to? Why wasn't she taken seriously? Jenny's concerns aside, any examination of assessment and classroom evidence revealed clear evidence of Donny's failure to learn. Why wasn't this taken seriously?

Jenny and Donny belonged to a social underclass. They were members of a cultural group referred to as "urban Appalachian," "Poor Whites" from the mountains or hills, "hillbillies," "white trash." Donny's failure to learn was not considered worthy of attention, and Jenny's inability to get herself heard was intimately related to this fact. Jenny wasn't taken seriously as a rightfully concerned mother because it is a deeply held belief, or stereotype, of the middle class that poor urban Appalachians are unfit as parents (Starnes, 1990). This stereotype prevented school personnel from interpreting her complaints and concerns in the same way they would interpret complaints and concerns from a middle-class mother. Donny's failure to learn *anything* was not noted because this was the expected pattern. Nothing to get excited about. What do you expect from these people? Happens all the time! That someone would care about this family was somewhat unsettling to the school.

Now, while this study is often cited as noteworthy because it focuses on poor whites instead of poor people of color, I want to suggest that this marginalization and denial of educational opportunity is not restricted to this urban Appalachian population. Rather, I see this study and the struggles and dreams it reveals as an up-close *example* of the devastation wrought by issues of class and power in all of our schools and in all of the countries of the world where clear underclass populations exist in illiterate or low literate and impoverished conditions. I am saying that insofar as the lower classes, the socially low-status peoples of this country fail to learn to read and write commensurate with their middle-class peers, there is not much difference between the United States of America and third-world countries. The issues are the same.

First, socially and politically marginalized people are held in disdain by those who hold the power. While they may be pitied and while many well-meaning middle-class people may volunteer clothes and money to help stave off the most devastating effects of poverty, there is always a generalized belief that they cannot learn as well as those in power—the middle/upper classes. It is believed that they "just don't have it" as far as intelligence and/ or the will to learn, to achieve, to move out of their impoverished conditions go. This disdain, this general stance of diminished expectations exerts a powerful and insidious effect on the education offered to marginalized people. I've referred to the effects on the education of Donny, and my book, *Other People's Words*, details this and describes similar effects on the education of Donny's mother and father (Purcell-Gates, 1995). In El Salvador, where I studied the literacy education of impoverished peasants (Purcell-Gates & Waterman, 2000), there was no real effort to offer schooling at all for the campesinos in the rural areas. Most of the patched-together schools with their seriously undertrained teachers were the result of volunteer operations run by various church organizations or social/political action groups. Yet meaningful and effective education is being offered to the middle and upper classes in the cities.

Second, language always seems to play a central role in this class-related denial of educational opportunity. This is undoubtedly because the language one speaks is the clearest and most stable marker of class membership, as George Bernard Shaw's *Pygmalion* demonstrated so entertainingly for us many years ago. While in some third-world countries, this means a completely different language spoken by the marginalized, in most, including the United States, it also means socially marked different dialects. I say socially marked because dialects of those in power do not elicit the same knee-jerk disdain and assumptions of deficit as do the dialects of the sociopolitically marginalized. For example, the Boston dialect of the Kennedys or the southern dialect of Jimmy Carter are never pointed to as evidence of cognitive and linguistic deficit. But let a poor, urban Appalachian woman speak for only a few minutes and powerful attitudes of prejudice and assumptions of inferiority are elicited. The vignette at the start of the article occurred when I was visiting Donny's classroom a year after the end of the study to observe his functioning. I introduced myself to his teacher and explained my interest in Donny. She conveyed her opinion of him and his school ability mainly through eye rolls, shrugs, and knowing grins. When I told her that I felt he had made great strides given the nonliteracy of his parents, she volunteered that she had met his mother, Jenny, and then added, "As soon as she opened her mouth, I *knew* she was ignorant!"

"As soon as she opened her mouth!" I knew exactly what this teacher meant. Jenny's dialect marked her immediately, within this context of a city where urban Appalachians make up the poorest and least successfully educated minority population, as unworthy, stupid, and of no real concern to teachers like her.

I have seen this same attitude and dismissal on Native American reservations in this country, in Israel toward the Palestinians, in England toward the lower classes and the immigrants, and in El Salvador toward the campesinos.

With these sociopolitically driven attitudes toward the language that people speak, think with, and learn with, is it any wonder that there is a class difference in learning and achievement? Particularly for literacy development, one of the first basic, driving concepts and experiences needs to be the realization that the *printed word codes language.* The negative attitude toward the spoken language of urban Appalachians is so strong in the cities that teachers regularly insist that students not speak or read orally unless they drop their dialect and use "standard English."

If you are forbidden to use your language to learn to read and write, if you are forced to speak differently when reading and writing, then you are in effect being closed off, or at least seriously impeded from accessing the world of print. Jenny described it powerfully for me one day when, after realizing that her words could be written down and read, she exclaimed, "I never read my *own* words before! I only copied other people words! I never knew that I could write my own!" It took me an incredible amount of effort to get little Donny to just try to encode his own words and to stop only copying from books. But when he finally did, he began his journey toward the world of the literate where he now resides, a real reader and member of the literate community.

What Schools and Teachers Can Do

There are several moves that schools and teachers can make to help erase the entrenched class differences in literacy achievement. These suggestions are made assuming that the sociopolitical world remains as it is, with some groups in power and other groups marginalized. My ultimate wish would be to erase this imbalance of power. However, until that occurs, I believe that we must not allow one more day to pass implicitly cooperating in the denial of educational achievement to significant portions of our citizens and fellow human beings. The recommendations I am going to make are not untried. They draw on my own work as a teacher and teacher of teachers, on the work of educators such as Marva Collins, the Black Panthers in the '60s and '70s who ran successful programs in the inner cities, the teachers described by Lisa Delpit who saw to it that their poor, African American children learned to read and write and to function successfully, the teachers in the illegal slave schools in this country before emancipation who brought precious literacy to children and adults held in bondage, and the public school teachers struggling and succeeding to educate poor minority children within the public schools today.

First, and most obvious, teachers and schools must accept, believe, and act upon the belief that *children of poverty are learners, have been learning since birth, are ready to learn at anytime, and will learn.* This crucial beginning stance on the part of teachers will help to ensure that any failure in the achievement of these children will lead to an examination of their instruction and not to a shrugging off of their futures. It will lead us to examine ourselves and ask ourselves what is wrong with the way we are teaching these children? What do they need to learn? There is no one answer to this; it depends on the children, their cultures, their previous experiences, their dispositions, and so on. In the case of young Donny, I, as his teacher, after assessing the lack of experience he had had with literacy in his life, needed to provide him with multitudes of experiences with people reading and writing, show him how he could connect with the world of print through his language and his thoughts, and explicitly point out to him the ways in which print coded the world he knew as well as "other people's worlds." I did the same for Jenny, working with her to make the connection between her words and other people's words.

On the wider level of the classroom, I observed a teacher for one year in an inner-city school serving African American children living in a large housing project. This African American teacher absolutely refused to accept poverty and its many consequences as excuses for her first-graders to fail to achieve. I watched her as day after day she exhorted, insisted, directed, ordered, and led her charges in learning to read and write. She never doubted for a minute that they could learn, and she never for a minute assumed that they could learn without her. It was sometimes hard for me, as a white middle-class person, to watch.

One scene stands out in my mind: a little girl who often came to school hungry, tired, and stressed. This one morning she kept falling asleep on her desk as the class was reading from their reading books together. Miss M. (the teacher) sharply told her to stay awake and follow along, but when her eyes closed and her head hit the desk for the third time, Miss M. insisted that she stand while she joined the other children in the oral reading. "*No one* in this class is going to sleep when they're supposed to be learning to read!" declared this teacher. And learn to read they did. The class mean on the California Achievement Test at the beginning of the year was in the 30th percentile, after a year of kindergarten, significantly below average and absolutely typical for a low-SES population. At the end of this first-grade year, the class mean was at the 55th percentile, well within the national average, with a good number of children above average and the lowest scoring child at the beginning of the year, reading at mid-first grade level. This achievement would not have happened without this teacher and her absolute belief that, yes, life was hard for these kids, but they *were* learners, they would learn, and it was her job to see that they did, in ways that worked for them.

Secondly, and as part of this stance of accepting the children as learners, it is necessary to accept their language as that with which they learn, and use that language to help them begin their education. It is the need to conceptually separate the process of learning to read and write from the sociopolitical issues surrounding language use. Nonstandard, socially marked dialects do prevent people from succeeding in the middle-class world, but they do not prevent people from learning to read and write. If we insist that learners learn a different way of talking and communicating before, or as a condition of, learning to read and write, we leave them irrevocably behind. No one "talks" like written language. Everyone uses fragmented syntax, different pronunciation patterns, and different types of vocabulary words when they talk as compared to when they read and write. The belief that educated people talk in complete, standard, syntactically integrated sentences is just wrong and ill informed. The concept of "sentence" as well as of "word" is a written language one. The "sound" system taught through phonics instruction never matches *anyone's* spoken language. The difference is that people with social and political capital get away with their "deviations," learn to adjust their language to the oral or written context, and are never made to believe that the way they talk is responsible for any failure to learn to read and write.

People without this social/political capital are told, as Jenny was, that they cannot learn to read because of the way they talk. "That's why it was hard for me to sound my words out," Jenny echoed her teachers. "Because I talk different; 'cause I'm, you know, countrified. And my words don't come out the way they're supposed to." When Jenny was shown that her knowledge of language could help her learn to read, that she did not have to say words the way the phonics system described the pronunciations, that what she had to do was to "sound out" to her dialect, then she could get a toehold on this process of learning to read. Miss M. never told the children in her first-grade class that they talked wrong. She did point out for them how the written language they were learning to read and write said things differently when syntax and vocabulary were involved. And she completely accepted their pronunciations of vowel and consonant sounds when they were learning to "sound out." I saw the same teacher attitudes and behaviors with the same successful results in literacy classes in El Salvador.

Third, we must realize that speakers will use the appropriate oral language register (or "type" or form) to fit the social context they find themselves in, if they know it. Similarly, writers will use the appropriate written register to fit the social context they are writing in, if they know it. In other words, when opening a book, a reader will call upon—"activate"—his knowledge of written language rather than oral language because a book is a written-language context. Knowing standard oral registers will not, by itself, help readers and writers with written registers. Readers must be familiar with written narrative language, for example, in order to read and write it easily and accurately. They must know the vocabulary choices that occur more frequently in written narrative (e.g., *entrance* as compared to *door*); they must be familiar with the syntactic constructions that mark written narrative from oral (e.g., *"Begone!" said the furious queen, throwing the mirror after the fleeing princess.* as compared to *The queen was really mad and threw the mirror at her and went like "Go away!"* which would be much more typical if one were relating the same information orally.) But because readers employ a "nonstandard" mode in oral discussion, it does not follow that they cannot learn other modes for written communication.

Origin of Language Knowledge

None of us is born knowing how to talk appropriately in church, in court, in school, in a group of friends, and so on. Similarly, none of us is born knowing how to write a personal letter, a story, a science report, an excuse note, and so on. We all have learned whatever we know about different language variants or registers by being with people who are using them. However, while we are absorbing language knowledge as it is being used, most of us also have benefited from being given explicit language knowledge by people who have it. Examples of explicit explanation of language conventions include such information as: "We don't use that word in church!" "When you meet Mr. Rogers, be sure to look him in the eye and say, 'Pleased to meet you, sir.'" "When you write a letter, always begin with 'Dear So and So' and put a comma after that before you go down to the next line and begin your first sentence." "An argumentative essay usually begins with your claim, then has about three to five paragraphs providing facts or opinions that support your claim, and ends with a concluding paragraph where you restate your claim and your reasons that support it."

These two sources of language knowledge—experience of language in use and explicit explanation of the language features that distinguish different types, or registers, of language—must inform the curricular decisions teachers make as they teach children to read and write. The children need to experience the many different types of written language in use, listening to it, observing its formation by the teacher, and then reading and writing themselves. In the process, the children need clear and unambiguous information about how language shifts and changes to accomplish different social and learning goals—how to form and how to read the different types of written language found in stories, poems, reports, personal narratives, information texts, and so on. Insuring these children the opportunity to learn about written language forms is essential to ensuring that they grow and develop as readers and writers.

Beyond "Linguicism"

Some people refer to the prejudicial stereotyping involved in blaming nonstandard speakers' oral dialects for their academic failures as "linguicism." I agree that the negative attitudes toward nonstandard dialects and the resulting misguided instructional attempts to change people's speech are based on misinformation and ethnocentricity just as are the other "isms" like racism, sexism, and ageism. And, like the other "isms," linguicism, especially as it impacts literacy development and educational achievement, is responsible for insidious social and political marginalization, resulting in blighted lives and unfulfilled opportunities for legions of people.

My greatest hope is that we can begin to move away from these old, uninformed notions about language and literacy. We must begin to comprehend and deal with the real issues involved in the failure of the schools to teach, to their fullest potential, the millions of children and adults from minority and low-socioeconomic communities.

REFERENCES

Purcell-Gates, V. and Dahl, K. (1991). Low-SES children's success and failure at early literacy learning in skills-based classrooms. *JRB: A Journal of Literacy* 23, 235–53.

———— (1995). Other people's words: The cycle of low literacy. Cambridge, MA: Harvard University Press.

———— (1996). Stories, coupons, and the TV guide: Relationships between home literacy experiences and emergent literacy knowledge. *Reading Research Quarterly* 31, 406–28.

———— and Waterman, R. (2000). *Now we read, we see, we speak: Portrait of literacy development in a Freirean-based adult class.* Mahwah, NJ: Lawrence Erlbaum Publishers.

Starnes, B. (January 1990). Appalachian students, parents, and culture as viewed by their teachers. *Urban Appalachian Advocate*, 1–4.

Taylor, D. (1985). *Family literacy: Children learning to read and write.* Exeter, NH: Heinemann.

PART THREE

Teacher Knowledge

The question is not what you look at, but what you see.

—HENRY DAVID THOREAU

CHAPTER 9

Topsy-Turvies:
Teacher Talk
and Student Talk

HERBERT KOHL

Noted teacher and author, HERB KOHL, describes the enormous impact language has on the school classroom. Students are very sensitive to the language of their teachers—the words, the tone, its trustworthiness—while teachers are insufficiently aware of how they are being heard and understood. Without this awareness, this "attunement," teachers may find that their students are hearing something quite different from what the teacher hears herself saying, or from what she had hoped to say. A classroom can unravel quickly when vigilant students detect insincerity, condescension, anti-Semitism, racism, or even fear and uncertainty. To avoid this, teachers need to do what Herb Kohl calls making a topsy-turvy. Teachers must analyze how they are presenting themselves and then make a 180-degree shift and construct how their students hear them. Teachers must listen to their students, and they must also listen to themselves being listened to. Not impossible, as Kohl points out, for "lovers do it all the time."

The opposite is beneficial; from things that differ come the fairest attunement; all things are born through strife.

— HERACLITUS

Teacher talk and student talk are essential components that determine the quality of learning in the classroom. When there is dissonance between them, other kinds of strife develop. When I first began teaching I didn't know how to speak to or with my students. Standing in front of a group of young people is a linguistic challenge. It is not merely a matter of what you say but of how your language is understood and how you understand the language of your students. It is not just a matter of how you present lessons or counsel your students. Language is an everyday, every minute matter and nuances of inflection, tone, modulation, and vocabulary are constantly at play in the interaction of students and teachers. There is an unarticulated linguistic sensibility that determines the nature and quality of interaction in the classroom. Teachers are listened to more than they usually think they are, though listening, understanding, and obeying are three different things altogether.

When I was teaching a combined kindergarten and first-grade class in Berkeley, one of the students kept her face turned away from me during class discussions. I waited for a moment when Julia and I could talk privately and asked her what was wrong—was I too loud or were there other problems in the class—and her response was that she was afraid of not knowing the right answer to a question. Even if she knew it, she said, she was afraid of my questions. Perhaps she was equally afraid of what she imagined to be my response.

This shocked me because I felt that I had created an open and giving environment where questions and answers can be seen as acts of exploration. I even had a sign on the wall proclaiming MAKE MISTAKES and encouraged the students to make interesting guesses without worrying about being correct. She had heard all of that but didn't believe me. School was about being right and if you weren't right then you'll be punished. And worse you could never know if you were right. It was up to what the teacher decided. It wasn't me that was making her face turn away but the very idea of school performance, of having to expose her knowledge or lack of it in front of the other children in the class. She didn't know where she would come out and was afraid to find out. I've been there a lot of times myself.

For Julia it was not a question of being wrong but never being sure in the presence of a teacher and classmates how you will look and whether you will be humiliated. I told her and it took a while for her to accept it, that intelligent guessing was more important than avoidance of learning.

In a way the story has two happy endings. Later that school year the class had to take the CBEST test. One question on the test showed a woman mopping the floor. The question was: She likes to: a) cop, b) hop, c) mop, and d) pop. Julia and the rest of the girls in the class refused to answer the question, informing me that she does not like to mop. They could read. They rejected the premises of the questions. And they felt that truth was stronger than testing. They were six years old.

What was I to do? Every one of those girls could read the question, knew the answer expected of them, and, because of our discussions on women's rights, their own family's commitment to women's liberation, and their own perceptions that women do not like to mop, decided not to answer a question designed by so-called experts in phonics. You might say that the students had said, phonics be damned.

My problem was not to coerce the students into answering a

question against their own conscience. I couldn't bring myself to do that. Rather it was whether to give them credit for an answer that I knew they could give if they chose. It was a question of whether I let them be punished for their own sensibilities or just fill in the right blank for them. If I did, would I be cheating for my students or would they be cheated by the nature of the test and the budding sophistication of their social awareness if I didn't do it?

Ultimately I decided to give them credit. Knowledge and intelligence is more important than conformity to the norms of testing. And the sensible revolt of young children when they are articulate and clear about the issue is a sign of the success of education, not its failure.

The second happy ending is that Julia and the other girls in the class are doing very well now that they are in their thirties. This one question on a high-stakes test was not important, but when talking to some of them, I've learned that the support they received, the validation of their thoughts and ideas, and the defiance of unreasonable authority have stood them well over the years.

School is a place of anxiety and strife for most students and achieving the fairest attunement that Heraclitus refers to is a complex matter involving language, patience, visceral perception, intuition, intelligence, and compassion. And on a minute to minute basis in the classroom, language is central to the development of attunement. Recently I was asked to sit in on a classroom for a few hours in the hope that I could provide some insights into why the teacher was having trouble with students learning and even paying attention. The teacher was young, highly motivated, and committed, even passionate, about his students learning.

Sitting in the back of a classroom when doing observations often has advantages. The children who'll be closest to you are the ones who either chose to sit in the back or were sent there. They are either the most indifferent or the most defiant. It's the cynical section of the seating arrangement. In the midst of the lesson one of the back-of-the-roomers turned to another and said, "There he goes again." The other just shrugged and put his head on the desk.

My response was to listen more carefully to how the teacher was talking. He was young and inexperienced, and he had not developed a tone or manner in the classroom that was easy and sincere. He was playing at being a teacher, speaking the way he imagined teachers should talk, looking above the heads of his students, not making eye contact, and pushing on with the lesson whether the students were understanding what he said or not. It was a function of his insecurity though, unfortunately, he saw it as the student's inability to pay attention. He needed what I have come to call a topsy-turvy.

Topsy-turvies are illustrations that when turned 180 degrees display two completely different images. For example, a topsy-turvy might look like a smiling woman from one perspective but when turned 180 degrees it might look like a nasty and angry pirate. It takes a lot of skill to make a convincing topsy-turvy. I have found that the concept of topsy-turvy provides a powerful metaphor that helps teachers transform their way of looking at themselves in the classroom. It is a matter of learning how to analyze the presentation of yourself in the classroom and then making a 180-degree shift and attempting to construct how your students see you. This implies an acceptance of opposition, of the idea that what you want as a teacher and what your students want or expect may be dissonant. It also requires the more personal and in many ways difficult integration of the idea that how you think you are speaking and how your students interpret what you are saying are not necessarily the same. The hard thing is talking to a whole class when people listen differently. Students interpret, reflect, analyze, and respond to the nuances of language in the classroom, and since most of the permitted language in the classroom is teacher talk, it is to that language that an excessive amount of student emotion and intelligence is committed.

It is essential to realize that this is not a matter of lack of caring or the will to help students. It is more a question of social and linguistic differences in a context where students and teachers are not hearing language in the same way. It is not just teacher talk that is problematic. Student talk has to be interpreted as well. This has nothing to do with language differences. It has everything to do with the way in which language is heard and interpreted, with tone, presentation, attitude, implication, and an understanding of how to convey complex meaning in a way that is understood by the spoken-to.

This places a burden on teachers, who are supposed to be the authorities in the classroom. The exchange of ideas, feelings, social understanding, and conversation in the classroom is fundamentally under the control of teachers unless the classroom is out of control. This is independent of teaching styles and pedagogical orientation. Language exists not merely on the level of words, sentences, paragraphs, dialects, accents, and linguistic differences. It is a social phenomenon that has complex personal implications relating to how the more formal aspects of reading, writing, and talking are interpreted on an everyday basis. It has to do with how things are said, how questions are asked or answered, and how much teachers and students listen to each other.

New teachers, if they do not come from communities that are similar to those they teach in, are particularly vulnerable to miscommunication. The students do not yet know or understand their teachers' style of talking. The teachers don't know how they are being heard. There is a lot of literature about learning style but not enough about teaching language and styles. The presentation of self in the classroom is a major part of the effectiveness of connecting with students and enhancing their learning. If you are too soft, too hard, too rigid, or too permissive, the students will develop attitudes that often contribute hostility or resistance to learning. And casual remarks can become defining moments in your relationship with your class.

Over the past few years, I have seen teachers tell students how much they love them and found out that some of the teachers didn't know all of their students' names. Young people are experts at understanding false pretensions of love and caring. After all, it's hard to love someone you don't really know. And if you say you love your students, then you can be sure that they will test that protestation of affection.

Recently I visited in a classroom where the children were out of control. I found them imaginative and ingenious in their strategies of defiance but found myself angry at them. I didn't love what they were doing to themselves and felt that they had developed dysfunctional school behavior that would end up hurting them in the future. The teacher, a very caring but inexperienced person, was screaming love at the children, saying how wonderful they were and how much she cared about them. Their response was cynical defiance and mockery. They were in control while they were out of control.

Students are very sensitive to the interface of language and behavior and learn how to listen selectively if they do not trust the teacher's language. They often ignore the words and listen for the tone. Teachers sometimes mistake this for the students not paying attention. However they usually are, though not necessarily to what the teacher intends.

I visited another classroom where the teacher took the opposite track and applied heavy and punitive discipline. The students' response was the same. There is a fine line between discipline and love that leads to good learning and creative teaching. Tough love makes no sense to me. The line I am talking about has to do with creating trust, respect, and a sense of teacherly identity. As a teacher it is essential to be an adult among young people. This may sound trivial or silly because it is hard to know what it means to be an adult. For me it has to do with passionate and loving authority and knowledge. You have to know what you are teaching, to learn how to understand your students both as individuals and as a group, and to fight against resistance to learning. You are not one of them, and you are being paid and they are required to attend. Teaching is a matter of craft, experience, and art, which makes teaching well a continuing challenge. Teachers' language and the nature of conversation in the classroom are determining factors in learning.

This implies that teachers should be aware of the major challenge of understanding how they are heard and not merely concentrating on how students speak and respond to teacher speech. Consciousness of the listener is hardly attended to in teacher education. It requires a topsy-turvy, an attempt to pay attention to how you are heard at the same time you are talking. Lovers do this all of the time. They speak to each other and worry about whether they are understood. Politicians do the same thing. They speak in order to win an audience, and if they are not conscious about how they are being understood, they will lose their audience. The same thing is true for actors in live theater where sensitivity to the audience helps shape the intensity and effectiveness of a performance.

Teaching is a performance. It doesn't make any difference whether you are teaching in a structured full-frontal teaching classroom or in a personalized environment where there is opportunity to work with students individually or in small groups. The way in which teachers speak shapes students' attitudes and is a major determinant in the nature and quality of the learning environment.

Small things—comments, questions, responses, phrases, tone—often make big differences in student attitudes, not merely toward their teachers, but toward what their teachers teach. Over the past few years I've been observing a number of young teachers in their classrooms. I know the students' and teachers' behavior were affected by my presence but not enough to conceal the nature of life and culture of the classrooms. What has been striking is the covert language of the children, and the struggles the teachers have to be taken seriously by their students. One dramatic example was in a fourth-grade classroom. The teacher, a young man with high motivation, love of children, and no experience living or working with children of color from poor communities, was struggling to give the class a homework assignment. About twelve of the twenty-five students paid attention. That was the core of the class that did the work he assigned and who often found themselves oppressed and harassed by other students who found the entire academic enterprise of the classroom irrelevant to their lives. Given his commitment to the learning of all of the students he rephrased the assignment, diagrammed it on the chalk board, and handed out clear instructions that a few of the recalcitrant students made into paper airplanes and threw around the classroom.

At last in a fit of anger caused by the frustration of not being able to teach or help people he knew needed his help, he exploded at one of the boys in the room. At that point another boy, clearly a leader, said, "Okay, Mr. Gold, we'll let you talk."

The students were aware of how the teacher was struggling to find a presence and language adequate to the authority the school's district had vested in him. It was a dysfunctional topsy-turvy— teacher authority and student power. The authority was neglected, the power misused. The students knew they were in control of language in the classroom.

There are areas of great linguistic sensitivity in the classroom, sensitivity that teachers have to think through carefully before they speak. As the children listen, their own experiences, beliefs, and understandings can often provoke crisis or prevent learning. In a classroom of predominantly Jewish children a discussion of Christ as the sole God can easily turn students against a teacher. Muslim students take offense to references to the Koran that the teacher does not know are considered heretical. A casual joke about Christ can also set off anger and defiance. Religion is a sensitive area to speak about in the classroom, as is race. The construction of a sensitive and yet natural and fluent teacher language is a challenge that beginning teachers have to struggle with.

A few years ago I observed another painful situation, one that I have faced over the years. Francisca, the teacher, had come from a middle-class Latino family, and had to deal with complex questions of racism, curriculum, and respect. She didn't know that all of these things are intimately bound in a complex fabric of language where you can pull out one thread and the fabric of the whole classroom will unravel.

It was about 1:45 in the afternoon in Francisca's class. The period had begun at 1:20. Things were going along well—about 60 percent of the students were interested in the project and the others were passive or asleep. The pain of seeing 40 percent of the kids disappearing in the classroom, something I have experienced more than any person should have to witness, was depressing me. There were kids who were not doing what the teacher wanted or just fading into their fantasies of life after and outside of schools.

An African American student (this was a sixth-grader) walked in halfway through the class, threw his bag on a table, and pushed a Latino student off a chair, laughed, and sat down on it.

I waited for the teacher's response.

Nothing.

Who was being damaged? Both students and the teacher, who was out of contact with the children she was teaching. My instincts told me she was afraid of them. There was no one at the school to support her. She was young and romantic and really cared to teach her students. She was committed to their learning and had not yet learned how to translate this into her language or work in the classroom, though she succeeded in gaining the necessary experience and self-confidence over her next years of teaching and now is a creative and effective teacher who knows how to talk to and with her students.

The youngster who had tossed his bag on a table came in with an attitude, and was at least a half hour late for the class. All of the other kids looked at the teacher since she had to deal with his comments on everything she said and the one was trying to teach. My temptation was to intervene but at that moment it would undermine her authority.

I watched. The class went on, the boy continued to disrupt the lesson. Finally she reached the point where she told the boy to shut up. A number of the girls in the class, all African American and Latina, just about cheered. But he turned to her and said, "Are you a racist? Do you hate black people?"

Francisca had a panicked look on her face. She didn't consider herself an overt racist, had studied racism and its manifestations in a college, had a keen sense of racial and social conflict in the United States and fell into the trap. "Yes," she said, "all non-black people are racist and I have had to deal with my own racism."

The girls who were on her side all of a sudden turned sympathetic to the boy who had caused the trouble in the first place. One muttered, "I don't want no racist teacher here," and got up to walk out. It took a lot of effort to bring the class under control, and, fortunately, the class bell rang before anything else developed.

This new teacher was in a classroom of eleven- and twelve-year olds, not in a semiotics or sociology class in college. Her language created hostility and rage she could not have anticipated and was not prepared to work with. This brings up two questions of language: when is it necessary to speak out, even in anger, about a student's behavior; and when is it essential to refuse to answer a question or evade it if it is clearly meant to insult you and disrupt the class.

Certainly there was a need to speak out against the boy's first action and not to let it pass in the hopes that things would settle down. It was also necessary at that point to support and console the boy who had been thrown off the chair.

There are different ways that the situation could have been dealt with. The teacher could have told the boy to leave and enter again, and restored the other boy to his seat. Alternately the teacher could have sent the boy to the principal or talked to him directly with the goal of having him apologize. What was imperative was a verbal intervention at the moment of offense, an acknowledgment of the attack and of the rights of the offended. The specific way this is done has to do with the structure of discipline in the classroom and, unfortunately, many beginning teachers do not feel comfortable with discipline. The mastery of some unambiguous language of discipline and the actions that accompany it are crucial aspects of the development of teaching skill.

On the other hand there are times when it makes sense to refuse to answer a question directly and fall into a trap a student sets for you. It is almost like taking the Fifth Amendment. It is probably true that all non-African Americans are racist in some way—personal or institutional. And it is possible to discuss that issue with students in a planned and well thought out way. But the challenge to Francisca was not intended to lead to a critical discussion of racism. Rather it was intended to throw the class into chaos. It is essential, if you are going to teach in a community in which you are a stranger, an "other," not to air your guilt and uncertainty in ways that give children illegitimate authority.

There were alternative responses that imply that sometimes avoidance, silence, or even sham are necessary to defuse a negative situation. For example, it would have been possible to say that it was essential to get on with the lesson and come back to the issue of racism in general in a few days. It would have been possible to ignore the question and tell the student he was speaking out of turn. Finally it would have been possible to answer "no" and get on with the business of teaching.

The boy realized that he had mobilized a linguistic battle which the teacher was unable to deal with at the moment and she responded out of her college intellectual experience rather than the exigencies of the classroom. Best perhaps would have been to use the avoidance strategy and then return to the issue at a future date when she was prepared and the students aware of the issue they were going to examine.

I remember my first revolt as a student. It was in 1949 at Junior High School 82 in the Bronx. I was in a combined seventh- and eighth-grade class. We had a wonderful teacher who was known and loved in the community. She retired in the middle of the school year and was replaced by a young teacher who was clearly motivated but inexperienced. The class, all of us, were either Jewish or Italian, and those days the struggle to create the state of Israel, the recovery from World War II, the Holocaust were in everyone's mind every day. The teacher was neither Jewish nor Italian, and definitely was not a New Yorker. I can still see her face and still feel guilt about what happened to her.

Her first goal was to shape us up but we were a gifted class and didn't need much shaping up. Her second goal was to keep us quiet. Anyone who has ever tried to teach Jewish and Italian kids knows that silence is not part of our repertoire. The third goal was to erase the memory of our retired teacher, which was a major strategic mistake. You celebrate the memory of people who are loved and try to move in their jet stream until you find your own way. Then you become an honored member of the community and can mobilize support.

However, this teacher started out by telling us how much more discipline-oriented she would be, how she would make us work harder, would not tolerate informal conversation in the classroom, and most of all, "would not let you people bring your cultural politics into the classroom."

In Jewish communities when people say "you people" it feels, smells, and sounds like anti-Semitism. Italians take that language the same way only in the context of their culture and society. Being a crossbreed I took it both ways.

On reflection I think this young teacher had the best of intents, had a program for us, and was trying to fit into a situation where she had to create respect and affection. But she didn't know us and had no insight into how we interpreted her words.

One afternoon a number of us met and decided to destroy her ability to teach us and chase her out of the class and the school. We did the same crazy thing I experienced in classrooms where I taught over fifteen years later. We fell off our desks when we didn't stand on them, refused to do any work, hid all of the text books, set off sophisticated stink bombs, and, in as many ways as our adolescent rebellion could imagine, made this poor woman's life miserable.

Naturally she called our parents. Unfortunately she made many of the same mistakes with our parents she had made with us.

A group of parents from our class went to meet her and she said, once again, "You people have disrespectful children." To call our parents "you people" was heard as an anti-Semitic statement and to imply that their children were *all* disrespectful was an insult to them as parents. I'm sure she did not know how she was being heard. It is not easy to develop a comfortable language to use in the classroom when you don't know much about your students, and it can be harder in a community when you are a stranger to it. This requires attention to how you are being heard and trying to listen to yourself through other people's ears.

We students got more shouting and some physical statements

from our families in the privacy of our homes. But the parents, as a group, many of whom were experienced union organizers and political activists, went to the principal and said, quite simply, "This teacher will not come back as she does not honor or respect us."

Our parents won but told us as students that the next teacher was going to be respected no matter what happened because we had longer lives than junior high school.

My JHS 82 experience has stood me very well, both in my own public school teaching and my current work with beginning teachers. Going back to the teacher I observed who opened up her insecurities to her students and ended up with a class out of control, it is probably true that all white people in the United States take in racism with their oatmeal; but it is not true that all white or Latino people always act based on racist sentiments. I don't know whether the junior high teacher we wiped out was actually anti-Semitic.

Teacher talk is central to the tone and nature of life and culture in the classroom. Overt racism simply cannot be tolerated but simple comments, attitudes, and support for institutionalized practices of racism are all understood by students as they try to piece together a picture of what the classroom holds for them. Recently I spoke with a number of high school students who had been engaged in an anti-racist program. They were talking to a group of teachers about how they listened in the classroom. One commented on how teachers talking to students about their futures often manifested racist attitudes by suggesting that some students weren't college material. Another one mentioned how a teacher told him how good he was doing in school and how proud she was that he was working up to potential. However he had a B− average. He heard these comments as racist and knew he could do better. I wonder how the teacher heard herself.

Teaching requires listening, not merely to your students but to yourself being listened to. Simple assumptions about who students are, what their experience has been and what their current conditions and motivations are all require "attunement." Teachers have to develop their listening skills and their talking skills more now than at any time I have personally known in education. How one speaks and how one hears are essential factors in how well one teaches.

Heraclitus said, "from things that differ come the fairest attunement." It is a question of translation, understanding, and strength. But in a major way it is also a question of language, communication, and the creative arbitration of differences. Just recently I had to re-attune myself. I had a lens transplant operation. The lens in my right eye was extracted and replaced by a plastic lens. I had to learn to see again and reconstitute a world through new eyes. My organic eye and my plastic eye are learning to work together. It was more a brain problem than a vision problem. The challenge was to reconstruct the visual world and live in it. A topsy-turvy in the sense that I had to see the world through new eyes and understand that the world could be turned upside down by something as simple as my eyes. The world didn't change. My vision did. I needed to integrate a changing visual sensibility. It was not a matter of going back to the way I used to see but of adjusting to a world somewhat familiar and thoroughly transformed. Quarters looked like nickels, apples seemed as big as grapes, and the redwoods around our house in Northern California got smaller. Topsy-turvies all the time and attunement all the time.

The same readjustment applies in education and in particular to beginning teachers who are seeing and talking from the other side of the desk for the first time. It is a question of keeping one's eyes in focus with the life around us. The way in which children feel they have to display themselves and speak in the classroom is essential to how they choose to perform in school. And the analysis and consciousness of your own language as a teacher is equally essential. How do you sound? How is anger expressed? Who is praised? How is failure expressed in front of the class? How are you exposed when you think you are failing or perhaps even in despair? How many times a week do you express joy or thanks sincerely felt rather than mechanically administered as a matter of educational policy? Where is your joy in teaching and how is that conveyed? To me these are the essential questions teachers must confront, not the questions of test scores or covering the curriculum. Teachers should be as resistant and resilient as their students and learn the fine art of defying ignorant authority intelligently. After all, at its best, teaching is a nurturing and militant vocation and a wonderful thing to be doing in cynical times.

When you see trouble, attune your work and topsy-turvy your practice in the service of your students. If you see your students failing, re-attune your work. Listen when you talk and understand that you are listened to as well as talking to your students. And sometimes laugh at the things you've said under pressure and share that laughter with your students and talk, talk, talk about how people speak and listen. We have to become a more literate society and I think literacy will not come through testing and an obsession with standards, but through patient, intelligent and sensitive speaking, reading, and listening.

Topsy-turvy thinking is not new. In 1701, within *A Modest Proposal*, Jonathan Swift wrote a short satire entitled "Meditation on a Broomstick" in which he said, "a broomstick . . . is an emblem of a tree standing on its head; and pray what is man, but a topsy-turvy creature, his animal faculties perpetually mounted on his rational, his head where his heels should be, grovelling on the earth! and yet, with all his faults, he sets up to be universal reformer and corrector of abuses, a remover of grievances . . . and raises a mighty dust where there was none before."

Teaching is a blessedly complex activity which requires complex and continual attunement, and in which the upside downs of topsy-turvy life in the classroom are one of the great joys and privileges of spending a life with children.

CHAPTER 10

Toward a National Public Policy on Language

GENEVA SMITHERMAN

Most of the pieces in this volume engage the issue of language discrimination directly, recounting its enormous cost in personal and educational terms. Knowing full well how lastingly destructive a teacher's intolerance can be, the nation's two largest organizations of English teachers—the National Council of Teachers of English (NCTE: representing elementary and secondary school teachers), and the Conference on College Composition and Communication (CCCC: a network of college professors) have tried to make a difference by playing a leadership role with their membership. In this 1986 piece, GENEVA SMITHERMAN addresses the NCTE and the CCCC with a direct and compelling call to action. Smitherman's challenge to these groups comes twelve years after both groups passed resolutions affirming the right of students to speak their own language.*

Just as those resolutions did not stem the tide of educational discrimination, so Smitherman's piece is another chapter in a frustratingly slow process. In 1988, the CCCC convened to reassess their 1974 policy in light of the growing English Only movement. They

---

*In 1974 the CCCC passed "The Students' Right to Their Own Language," which affirmed the right of students to their own patterns and varieties of language and dialect, as well as speaking style. Teachers must be trained to respect diversity in order to uphold this right and preserve the heritage of dialects, the document asserted. The NCTE passed a similar policy that same year—Convention Resolution #74.2.

supported a principle of "English Plus," which became formally known as the National Language Policy of 1988. The components of this policy are outlined in Smitherman's article. In 2000, a survey was conducted of all members of NCTE and CCCC to assess how widely the groups' policies have taken effect. Although the survey was confined to the organizations' members—those teachers most likely to identify with agreed-upon policy statements—65 percent of the respondents were not familiar with the 1974 "Students' Right to Their Own Language," and 66 percent had no knowledge of the more recent National Language Policy passed in 1988.

"Toward a National Public Policy on Language" calls for a straightforward, active approach from these professional groups. As the results of their 2000 survey and the lived experiences of the contributors to this volume testify, there is much work left to be done.

Darlene tryin to teach me how to talk. . . . Every time I say
something the way I say it, she correct me until I say it
some other way. Pretty soon it feel like I can't think. My
mind run up on a thought, git confuse, run back and sort of
lay down. You sure this worth it? I ast. She say Yeah. Bring
me a bunch of books. Whitefolks all over them, talking bout
apples and dogs. What I care bout dogs? I think. . . . But I
let Darlene worry on. Sometimes I think bout the apples and
the dogs, sometimes I don't. Look like to me only a fool
would want you to talk in a way that feel peculiar to your
mind.

— CELIE, IN *THE COLOR PURPLE*
(Walker 1982)

With Celie's profound philosophical statement in backdrop,
I am here issuing a challenge to speech, language and composition
professionals to take the leadership role in working toward a national public policy on language. The immediate impetus for this
call to action comes from the precipitously declining rates of literacy and educational achievement in Afro-American communities.
For example, school drop-out rates are running about 65 percent
in Chicago and 66.5 percent in Detroit, both urban school districts
with overwhelmingly large Black student populations. However,
the policy would govern language teaching and language use
throughout the U.S. and ultimately would be beneficial to *all* communities. Thus, as has always been the case throughout U.S. history, whenever Blacks have pioneered social change, the result has
been change and betterment throughout the American social re-

ality. Recall, for instance, how the movement for Black Power
ushered in calls for Brown Power, Red Power, Female Power, Student Power, Counterculture Power, Grey Power, and on and on—
the Black struggle in the 1960s and 1970s opened up the economic
and social structures for *everybody*.

... It is time to call the children in and teach them the lessons
of the Blood. ...

In 1974, the Conference on College Composition and Communication passed a policy resolution, "The Students' Right to Their
Own Language." I am honored to have been a part of the movement behind this resolution and later a member of the committee
that wrote the expanded document accompanying the resolution
(Butler 1974). Our goal at that time was the promotion of such a
policy throughout the profession of speech, language and composition scholars and educators. Unfortunately, that goal was not realized.

In 1977, I wrote that "ultimately teachers should struggle for a
national public policy on language which would reassert the legitimacy of languages other than English, and American dialects
other than standard" (Smitherman 1977). Unfortunately, that goal
was not realized.

In 1979, in *King v. Ann Arbor* (Smitherman 1981), Judge
Charles C. Joiner issued a ruling reaffirming the legitimacy of
Black English and the existence of its African sub-stratum and
mandated that the Ann Arbor School District "take in account"
Black English in the educational process of teaching Black Children
to "read in the standard English of the school, the commercial
world, the arts, science, and professions" (Joiner 1979). Thus, the
King decision laid the basis for instituting a language policy for
the Black community that would have had far-reaching implications for other communities. Unfortunately, that goal was not realized.

Although linguist Wayne Williams applauded my work and that
of my colleagues in *King*, nonetheless, he argued that from a policy

standpoint, the "Black English Case" may have been "premature" (Williams 1982). However, I say to my fellow linguist, Brother Williams, that recent movements against linguistic minorities and the alarming school drop-out rate among black English-speaking underclass serve to remind us that the motion of history does not wait for political maturity.

Because we failed to act, now we must re-act. The aborted movement, spear-headed by the Conference on College Composition and Communication, to establish a national public policy on language would have addressed the mother tongue and language crises of *all* Americans—not just Blacks, Browns, Reds. "The Students' Rights to Their Own Language," after all, reaffirmed the language rights of White Appalachian students, female students, Arab students, White counterculture students, middle-class students—in short, *all* students. For you see, no one escapes the tentacles of the self-appointed guardians and preservers of the national tongue (as spoken by themselves, I remind you). Witness, for example, the castigation of President Reagan when he said in his 1985 Inaugural Address, "If not us, then who?" meaning, "If *we* do not make the hard decision, then who will? (in which case, according to the long arm of linguistic law, Reagan should have said, "If not we, then who?") In his *New York Times* language column, William Safire defended Reagan's right to his own language and took the President's detractors to task for insisting on such formal and "laughably stilted" usage (Safire 1985). While the powerful, such as Reagan and others of his ilk, don't need linguistic sanctuary, the less powerful among us do. Thus a policy affirming the mother tongue language and dialect of ALL would have the effect of protecting the many from the linguistic imperialism of the few.

All that is required for oppression to take hold is for good and well-meaning folk to do nothing. A language leadership vacuum has been created by the absence of national policy action from the professions and from political progressives. Into that vacuum have stepped reactionary and counter-progressive forces and movements. An illustrative case is "U.S. English." Some may dismiss this move-

ment as the folly of an erring and aging self-hating Japanese se-
manticist. But that would be folly, for S. I. Hayakawa's campaign
to amend the U.S. Constitution to make English the official language has succeeded in creating a burgeoning, highly effective and
increasingly mass movement, a linguistic corollary to the reactionary mood of conservatism reemerging across America. U.S. English
is a well-financed national organization, headquartered in Washington, D.C., which distributes a newsletter called *Update*. The
Constitutional amendment that Hayakawa introduced into the U.S.
Senate is currently being refined in a Senate committee which has
done a significant amount of work on the proposed amendment
already. Undoubtedly, U.S. English is primarily responsible for the
proposal in California to overturn the tradition of printing election
ballots in languages other than English. Such a proposal, if successful, would, of course, effectively disenfranchise large numbers
of Spanish-speaking voters who are on the verge of becoming the
dominant population in that State. Moreover, a movement like U.S.
English provides another justification for cutbacks in Federal fund-
ing for the language-based educational programs for Blacks and
other minorities struggling against functional illiteracy in school
districts across this country.

. . . It is time to call the children in and teach the lessons of the
Blood. . . .

I am proposing that speech, language and composition professionals
take up the unfinished business of the Committee on the Students'
Right to Their Own Language, bring to fruition the implications
of the *King* decision, and move quickly to counteract those reactionary sociolinguistic forces that would take us back to where
some folk ain't never left from. In calling for a national policy on
language, I take as theoretical framework the policy and planning
models of Fishman (1972, 1980); LePage (1964); Bamgbose (1976);
and Alleyne (1982). I shall use the terminology proposed by Fishman, the "language of wider communication," to refer to standard
American English.

I propose a three-prong policy—a 360° Trinity that constitutes an inseparable whole.

1. Reinforce the Need for and Teaching of the Language of Wider Communication

The teaching of the language of wider communication has never been an issue (though I for one have erroneously been accused of rejecting its teaching). It has never been an issue, *if* and *when* it has been promoted as an integral part of a policy that includes recognition, use and acceptance of the native tongue.

Among speech, language and composition professionals, there is plenty of evidence that this has not been the case. For example, in our analysis of the essays of Black students from the National Assessment of Educational Progress (Smitherman and Wright 1983), we found significant correlations between the frequency of Black English and the rater's score, i.e., the more Black English, the lower the score. This correlation existed even in the body of essays in which raters were instructed to look only at rhetorical features, that is, to use primary trait scoring to assess how well the student writer had mastered the rhetorical modality under evaluation. Yet, many of the essays rated high were deplorably devoid of content, meaning and message, and further, the frequency of Black English was generally quite low—generally less than 20 percent Black English forms in any given linguistic category. Quite apart from the distribution of Black English in the essays, the writers experienced difficulty in coping with the demands of the assignment and writing toward the topic. For example, some students, in very edited American English syntax, would shift topic and focus right in the middle of the essay.

It must be stressed, then, that emphasis on the language of wider communication is toward the use of language as power; not mere "correctness," but the use of language to "make the impossible possible."

The language of wider communication is the language of literacy and technology, as well as the medium in which even the historical experiences and lessons of the Blood have been captured. Thus there is no question, nor has there ever been any question, about the need for linguistic competence in this language. If to-day's speakers of non-mainstream languages and dialects are rejecting the teaching of standard English, if indeed, as Labov (1985) has suggested from his recent Philadelphia study, Black English is diverging from the language of wider communication, particularly among the Black underclass, it may be, in large measure, because educational institutions have never seriously accepted the mother tongue of the speech community. They've paid lip service to it, but they have not really accepted it. As James Baldwin said, in his *New York Times* essay, "If Black English Isn't a Language, Then Tell Me What Is?", published two weeks after the *King* decision:

> Now, no one can eat his cake, and have it too, and it is late in the day to attempt to penalize black people for having created a language that permits the nation its only glimpse of reality, a language without which the nation would be even more *whipped* than it is. . . . It is not his language that is despised; it is his experience. A child cannot afford to be fooled. A child cannot be taught by anyone whose demand, essentially, is that the child repudiate his experience, and all that gives him sustenance, and enter a limbo in which he will no longer be black and in which he knows that he can never become white. Black people have lost too many black children that way.   (Baldwin 1979)

. . . It is time to call the children in and teach them the lessons of the Blood. . . .

2. Reinforce and Reaffirm the Legitimacy of Non-Mainstream Languages and Dialects and Promote Mother Tongue Instruction as a Co-Equal Language of Instruction along with the Language of Wider Communication

The mother tongue language or dialect, of course, will vary according to the speech community. The point is that the indigenous language is the authentic voice of the speech community, and, as such, can establish the firm foundation upon which to build and expand the learner's linguistic repertoire. What Williams termed the "language conscious hypothesis" (Williams 1982) has been shown to have a great deal of validity. In Williams's own research in the Seattle, Washington, Black community, he demonstrated that Blacks who were conscious of their own language as a legitimate system were more receptive to learning the language of wider communication. As Bamgbose and other non-Western scholars have taught us, the mother tongue may be the only "passport to literacy" for the great majority of Third World schoolchildren. Certainly this appears to be the case for speakers of Black American English. For example, Pearson's work (1985) indicated that Blacks more fluent in Black speech acts, such as sounding and the Dozens, tended to be more fluent in the figurative, literary forms of the language of wider communication. Similarly, Simpkins and Holt's (1976) research with the *Bridge* materials demonstrated the feasibility and success of using Black English as a bridge to understanding and reading the language of wider communication in that some of the students in their experimental research program advanced as much as two years in reading level after one semester's exposure to the "bridge approach."

Finally, reaffirming the legitimacy of non-mainstream languages and dialects is critical if we are to bridge the developing divide and class tensions between the "have's" and "have not's" in Black and minority communities and between those minorities and Whites.

3. Promote the Acquisition of One or More Foreign Languages, Preferably a Language Spoken by Persons in the Third World, Such as Spanish, Because of Its Widespread Use in This Hemisphere

The educational benefits to be derived from foreign language study have to do with sharpening critical thinking and heightening verbal skills. In times past, one was not considered truly educated unless he/she commanded a foreign language. The excruciating and embarrassing narrowness of the American populace in language matters is illustrated in the following joke:

> What do you call a person who speaks three languages?
> Answer: Trilingual
> What do you call a person who speaks two languages?
> Answer: Bilingual.
> What do you call a person that speaks one language?
> Answer: An American.

Most importantly, it is imperative that Americans—of whatever color, race or sex—be enlightened about world cultures: sensitivity through language is one way to achieve such enlightenment. Contemporary history is rife with the sordid remains of narrow provincialism emanating from a world superpower (e.g., the Vietnam War). Our students, the citizens of the future, must be capable of understanding and, hopefully, of carrying on dialogue with non-Western peoples—the majority population in today's world.

There are several pragmatic moves necessary to make the policy outlined here a workable reality.

First, speech, language and composition professionals must work on the political front, in whatever way they can, to insure that, for instance, jobs and services are available for all, and especially for those we are teaching in our ebony and ivory towers. Acquisition of the language of wider communication, as Fishman tells us, must provide entrée to power and resources, or there is little reason for indigenous populations to adopt it. Further, as Alleyne cautions us, we should try to profit from the tragic history of several newly independent countries who have undergone linguistic and cultural transformation but who have not achieved modernization of the means of production or economic self-sufficiency—in short, they are still poor. And thus, in many Third and First World countries, the masses are rejecting technology and literacy campaigns.

Similar circumstances prevail in this country. For instance, in Black communities, intuition and logic suggest—if Labov's methodology, which some have labeled flawed, does not—that Black underclass communities are becoming speech communities whose language is increasingly diverging from the language of wider communication, as spoken by *both Whites and Blacks.* Of what benefit, one may well ask, is the language of wider communication to a community in which, for example, 75 percent of its youth from 16 to 24 years of age are unemployed—and unemployable, without some kind of massive economic intervention? Given the poverty and class powerlessness of such a community, linguistic differences are easily predictable.

To insure rewards from language and literacy for America's working and UNWORKING classes, speech, language and composition professionals should align with political progressives in demanding the restoration of budget cuts from education and other domestic programs and in opposing the military build-up and its gross and offensive budget. In general, then, we as professionals should take an active role in the political affairs of the country.

Secondly, we should work with other professions and organizations to promote the call for a language policy and to garner the political support for it in the public domain. Groups like foreign language teachers' associations, psychologists' associations, Children's Defense Fund and others all have a stake in a national public policy on language.

As a third step, speech, language and composition professionals are the ideal group to conduct the language awareness campaigns needed to accompany the movement for a language policy. These campaigns would be geared toward combating the myths about language use. Campaigns would be conducted through newspapers, television, and radio programs, magazines and in other popular media, in community forums, churches, and throughout the general public domain. The objective would be to combat the myths and misconceptions about both non-mainstream languages and the language of wider communication. Language standards do change, and attitudes about language change also. While Safire's approval of Reagan's "If not us, who?" is a dramatic example, it is only one of many such changes in attitudes about usage. In the case of Black English, for example, Linn (1982) has suggested that attitudes toward Black English are more positive than a decade ago. Intelligent speculation suggests that this may be the legacy of the Black Pride Movement of the 1960s and 1970s, which ushered in the widespread adoption of language, dance, music and other cultural forms from the Black speech community. We should capitalize on this healthy transformation of American language standards and extend it further.

Finally, we should work with the public schools to develop uniform standards and guidelines for linguistic performance. This kind of institutional collaboration is vital not only to the promotion of a language policy but also for the general education of our students. At least two states are currently involved in this kind of educational collaboration—California, through its focus on the educational underachievement of the State's linguistic minorities; and Ohio, through its Urban Initiatives Action Program for Language Education spearheaded by Central State University. Speech, language and composition professionals should all work collectively from preschool through graduate school on matters of language, literacy and standards of effective and successful uses of language. A vivid illustration of the need for this kind of educational cooperation is presented in a recent Georgia court case. Professor Jan Kemp filed a suit against the University of Georgia after she was fired for protesting the University's lowering of academic standards for its athletes and wealthy donors' sons. Reacting to the court ruling in Kemp's favor, John Thompson, basketball superstar Patrick Ewing's former coach at Georgetown, put it best:

> Of course there are things wrong with athletics . . . but if you want to look at the real scandal, look at the entire educational system . . . It wasn't a coach who passed these kids from grades one through six when he wasn't able to read . . . What about all these kids who can't read who AREN'T playing basketball or football?   (Wilbon 1986)

To summarize, the language policy proposed here has three inextricable parts: 1) reinforce the language of wider communication; 2) promote and extend the legitimacy of mother tongue languages and dialects; and 3) promote the acquisition of one or more foreign languages, preferably those spoken in the Third World. Such a policy is not only concomitant with the emerging pedagogy that language is the foundation stone of education; this kind of policy is also a basis for participation and leadership in world affairs.

. . . . It is time to call the children in and teach them the lessons of the Blood. . . .

REFERENCES

Alleyne, Mervyn C. *Theoretical Issues in Caribbean Linguistics.* Mona: University of the West Indies, 1982.

Baldwin, James. "If Black English Isn't a Language, Then Tell Me, What Is?" *New York Times*, July 29, 1979. Also reprinted in Smitherman, 1981.

Bamgbose, Ayo. "Introduction: The Changing Role of the Mother Tongue in Education." In Bamgbose, A., ed., *Mother Tongue Education: The West African Experience.* Paris: Unesco Press, 1976, pp. 9–26.

Butler, Melvin, ed. *Students' Right to Their Own Language.* Urbana: National Council of Teachers of English, 1974.

Fishman, Joshua A. *Language and Nationalism.* Rowley: Newbury House, 1972.

————. "Bilingual Education, Language Planning and English." *English Varieties World-Wide*, I:1 (1980): 11–24.

Holt, Grace, and Simpkins, Charlesetta. *Bridge.* Boston: Houghton Mifflin, 1976.

Joiner, Charles C. "Memorandum and Opinion," in Smitherman 1981.

Labov, William. *The Increasing Divergence of Black and White Vernaculars.* National Science Foundation, 1981–1984. Complete report available from the author: William Labov, Linguistics Laboratory, University of Pennsylvania, Philadelphia, Pennsylvania.

LePage, Robert B. *The National Language Question: Linguistic Problems of Newly Independent States.* London: Oxford University Press, 1964.

Linn, Michael. "Black and White Adolescent and Pre-Adolescent Attitudes Towards Black English," *Research in the Teaching of English* (1982): 16: 1, pp. 53–69.

Safire, William. "The Case of the President's Case," *New York Times*, March 10, 1985.

Simpkins, Gary. *Cross-Cultural Approach to Reading.* University of Massachusetts Ph.D. Dissertation, 1976. *Dissertation Abstracts International*, 1976, 37/09A, p. 5669 (University Microfilms, No. DCJ77-06404).

Smitherman, Geneva. *Talkin and Testifyin: The Language of Black America.* Detroit: Wayne State University Press, 1986. Originally published by Houghton Mifflin, 1977.

————, ed. *Black English and the Education of Black Children and Youth.* Detroit: Center for Black Studies, 1981.

————, and Wright, Sandra. "Black Student Writers, Storks and Familiar Places: What Can We Learn from the National Assessment of Educational Progress?" Final Research Report, National Council of Teachers of English Research Foundation, Urbana, Illinois. Also available from Geneva Smitherman, Center for Black Studies, Wayne State University, Detroit, Michigan.

Taylor-Delain, J., Pearson, P. D., and Anderson, R. C. "Reading Comprehensions and Creativity in Black Language Use: You Stand to Gain by

Playing the Sounding Game," *American Educational Research Journal* 22 (1985):155–74.

Walker, Alice. *The Color Purple*. New York: Harcourt, Brace, 1982.

Wilbon, Michael. "Thompson: Education a Problem." *Washington Post*, February 21, 1986.

Williams, Wayne. "Language Consciousness and Cultural Liberation in Black America." Paper delivered at the Sixth Annual Conference of the National Council for Black Studies, Chicago, March 1982. Available from the author: Center for Afro-American Studies, University of Washington, Seattle, Washington.

CHAPTER 11

The Clash of "Common Senses": Two African American Women Become Teachers

SHUAIB MEACHAM

Colleges and universities across the country are recruiting African American students to become teachers. SHUAIB MEACHAM suggests that these efforts will not be successful if the teacher education programs do not examine their attitudes toward Black English. Linda and Tanya are young African American women preparing to be teachers, and the process itself becomes harrowing. Linda, who grew up speaking Black, or African American, English has been inspired to go into education by one of her own teachers—a "true teacher." She finds, however, that the "common sense" (generally accepted practice) of teacher preparation is "standard form, standard grammar, Standard English" and that the language she speaks, the language that her very supportive family and all her friends speak, is deemed deficient. Tanya, on the other hand, grew up speaking Standard English, which she herself defines as "talking white." For Tanya, finding her place in the teacher education program is complicated by what becomes a vigorous struggle to maintain her own sense of cultural identity as a Black Woman.

According to James Baldwin, the one predictable constant within the considerable chaos of American identity is that those things "Black," or of Black cultural origin, are at the bottom of the social order. That is why the Ebonics controversy of 1996 struck so deeply. The Oakland School Board's Standard English Proficiency Program (SEP), by suggesting that Black language be used as an educative tool, an enhancement for learning, threw America's common sense into turmoil. That which America regarded as most lowly, the school board dared to elevate to a prominent place in the schools. The connection between Black language and schooling, specifically Black language and teaching, led to one of the most hysterical and utterly misinformed social debates in the history of American education. Notwithstanding the SEP program's previous success in using Black language to teach standard English and to raise standardized test scores, the country simply could not tolerate so violent a challenge to its common sense belief that Black culture and Black language had nothing to offer the educative process.

The country has been willing, however, to consider one culturally influenced means of closing the achievement gap between White children and children of color that has consistently plagued the educational enterprise. The idea that teachers of the same background as their culturally diverse students might be more effective in reaching them academically has gained some mainstream acceptance. Thus, many universities and colleges are recruiting more African American and other teacher candidates of color. These efforts, however, lead to some very profound dilemmas, given mainstream common sense that devalues Black culture and language.

Institutions that recruit teacher candidates from culturally diverse backgrounds have failed to ask important questions. For example, is the "common sense" (or "generally accepted practice") regarding issues of culture and language in the teaching profession the same as that held by culturally diverse teacher candidates? If not, how do teacher education institutions respond? Does the teacher education program attempt to accommodate different language dispositions, or does it demand that African American and other teacher candidates of color change their language and language attitudes to reflect the mainstream common sense? If the latter, what does such an attempt at change mean for the African American student teachers? And perhaps most importantly, do the assumptions of the teaching profession socialize Black teacher candidates *out* of the cultural and linguistic dispositions which would make them more effective with Black children?

These issues of common sense and its differing forms, professional choice, and cultural integrity, come together in the teacher education experiences of Linda and Tanya, two African American female teacher candidates. In the following pages I tell their story. Through their experiences, we may begin to identify ways of helping African American, as well as other non-mainstream teacher candidates, maneuver through the dangerous territory of two conflicting conceptions of cultural and linguistic reality. It is my hope that this paper will also allow teacher education institutions to understand the painful and potentially destructive consequences of ignoring the "clash of the common senses."

Cornel West has asserted that the most effective forms of Black resistance to the pervasive negative judgments regarding Black identity and academic potential have been those rooted in Black self-love. In other words, even in a society which presupposes that— by definition—that which is Black is flawed, Black self-love has enabled African Americans to thrive. African Americans, in the home, church, and community, have attempted to teach their children to love who they are—their flesh, their voice, their hair, their history. Black self-love has functioned as a kind of fortress against the constant attacks on Black humanity so prominent in American society.

When I first saw Linda, she stood out as awkward and vulnerable, the way that so many Black children appear against the background of the mainstream. With her dyed hair, Afrocentric tee shirts, and long, curling fingernails, Linda contrasted sharply with the sober, Midwestern attire of her teacher education classmates. Yet, beneath the appearance of difference and displacement, Linda was deeply rooted in educational achievement through her strong connections to a loving Black family and community.

Linda is a young woman from a working-class urban African American community. Traditionally, college students from working-class backgrounds are depicted as exceptions to the rule of their community life. Like the brilliant janitor in the movie *Good Will Hunting*, working-class students are portrayed as having to resist their surroundings and to leave their communities to realize educational achievement. In much educational research, African Americans are said to be particularly resistant to educational achievement as a group. Linda's story, however, is very different from that common conception. Linda is the product of an extremely nurturing and educationally supportive working-class African American community. Her family and community functioned as a kind of cultural womb, which nourished her with educational reinforcements and role models, and protected her from the negative valuations of the White mainstream. This educational support was not provided in Standard English, but in Black or African American English. This language was such a pervasive aspect of Linda's experience, that she was only vaguely aware of the fact that she spoke a distinctive code of speech. Therefore, in contrast to the mainstream common sense connection between Black language and educational failure, Linda's story combines Black language with educational motivation and achievement.

In an interview, Linda describes the way in which African

American working-class youth reinforce with each other the importance of attending college.

> *Linda:* Everybody went to some type of college. Whether it
> was a junior college to start off with or ...
> *Shuaib:* You mean your friends, let's say the 128th St. area?
> *Linda:* Oh OK ... Some of the ones that I hung with real
> close, yeah they even went to colleges. One went to Iowa;
> one went to Chicago State. Pretty much so. I'd say that
> everybody went.
> *Shuaib:* Why do you think so many people went?
> *Linda:* Everybody's goin, you know what I mean. I know
> Black people are not where they should be. You know, but
> there's more pressure put on it. It's like everybody has
> more people goin, you know, like their cousin mighta went,
> an older cousin, and they come back and they get to ex-
> perience theirs. So you know, before where you mighta
> gone into the army, you pass that along, people are now
> more aware of what's goin on if they got in school.

In spite of the specific reference to "school," the meaning of school which Linda and her peers applied to the college experience was far from traditional. In contrast to the traditional conception of the school as a place of mainstream conformity, Linda and her peers saw school as a place to meet their needs as young African Americans. Linda referred to college as a place to have the "Black experience":

> All my friends had graduated, my cousins and them, they all
> went to Black colleges. They said I could have a different
> experience, the Black experience. "You know, you'll have so
> much fun. You'd be in the South you'd be on your own ba-
> sically." So I went on and went to Clark ... But then they
> used to press you not to go to none of these White colleges.
> But I mean it's OK as long as you are who you are where
> you at.

The Black experience is a place set apart from the mainstream for the purpose of cultivating an alternative framework of common sense, a common sense based upon African American cultural needs. Linda spent one year at Clark. During that year, she was immersed within the Black experience and the African American cultural common sense which it fostered. In this common sense African American concerns were central, and permeated the college experience:

> The Black experience is when you get a lot of unity, a lot of political movements. You know things like marching against the KKK, Martin Luther King Day, they had big parades... They had an issue about light Blacks discriminating against each other... And then going to school. You just get with all of your people from all over, Chicago, New York, California wherever. You're gettin everybody from everywhere, different.... I guess all that is supposed to be the Black experience.... Supported by things like the United Negro College Fund, private donations, you know if the alumni came back and gave. People like Bill Cosby, Oprah Winfrey, they gave money... All of that could be a part of the Black experience.

A fundamental part of Linda's "Black experience" was the teaching which she encountered. The perception of teaching she experienced at Clark University was very different from what she might have found in the White mainstream. Whereas, in the mainstream, the teacher's responsibility is to promote White middle-class mainstream consciousness, the teacher in Linda's Black experience sets out to promote African American cultural well-being. This model of teaching, and its cultural common sense, motivated Linda to enter the teaching profession. The influence is evident in her description of a "true teacher" she encountered in college:

> I had always thought about being a teacher. But what kind of influenced me was a true teacher I had. He said that he

coulda come out and did a lot of things to make more money. But he felt that he was obligated to come back and teach those kids. And he was one of the ones to say that no matter what things we had to do that day, he would talk about Black issues. . . . It just really made me want to go back and teach in the inner city for a while.

Although it may seem that this conception of the Black experience is situated primarily within Black College settings, Linda described similar influences in educational settings prior to college. In fact the college teaching that Linda described is similar to patterns which Michele Foster, a scholar in the area of African American teaching, has identified throughout African American history at a variety of age levels. African American teachers, knowing the kinds of hostile conditions and circumstances their students would face, prepared them with an alternative conception of common sense, one which validated their cultural identities, histories, and future possibilities. This practice is captured in Linda's description of a teacher's actions during her elementary school years. The teacher deliberately deviated from lessons in order to culturally support his young students:

Now one of my Catholic schools had a Black teacher. He did, he would shut his door every day and he talked about Black history. Of course, they wanted you to only talk about it in February. But he'd talk about it every day. And he'd shut his door when he did it. Of course, it wasn't part of the lesson plan.

Linda was the first person in her family to attend a four-year post-secondary institution. In some respects this fact suggests that Linda was an exception to her family history. Behind that fact, however, there is a tradition of effort toward the attainment of a college education. Linda is not an anomaly within her family. Rather, Linda is a fulfillment of her family's educational aspirations. As such, Linda was celebrated for her accomplishments:

My grandmother had nine kids. Only one daughter dropped out, but as far as my mother and my aunts and them, all of 'em went like to junior colleges and they never got as high as an associate degree. So they really pumped college up. So like after my freshman year, I mean every time I came home, you know it was like, you know they was always sittin and stuff. I was the first one to go. So I was like being put on a pedestal. They was always callin me and takin me out, or something like that. . . . They would just buy me things. They would say things like, "As long as you're in school, there's nothin we won't do for you," things like that. So they was just proud.

The mainstream expectation is that those African Americans who enter higher education conform to mainstream standards. However, Linda, in her dress, her personal bearing, and most significantly, her use of African American English, did not conform and did not perceive any need to conform. The support from Linda's family and community enabled her to regard herself without any sense of educational deficit. Although she was vaguely aware of the fact that she sometimes spoke what she referred to as "slang" in informal settings, Linda saw herself as fully capable of achieving at the highest levels. The eventual confrontation between Linda's self-concept and the common sense of the teaching profession would profoundly shape Linda's experience of teacher education.

In contrast to Linda, Tanya assimilated into the teacher education program in both appearance and behavior. She wore the plain tee shirts and denim common throughout the university. Her hair, long and braided, complemented her café au lait skin tone and gave her the appearance of Egyptian royalty. While Tanya's physical dress blended in with her White peers, she was very outspoken and political in discussions and other interactions. Tanya frequently took up issues of cultural diversity that the program did not address. Her willingness to speak out and take on discrepancies between her own educational perspectives and that of the teacher education program's also reflected Tanya's experience of Black self-love. Whereas Linda's experience of Black self-love was one that insulated her from mainstream expectations, Tanya's family cultivated Black self-love of cultural self as an armor and a weapon with which to struggle actively against the White mainstream.

Tanya's preparation for cultural struggle, however, possessed an element of contradiction which troubled her deeply. Throughout her childhood, she had been admonished by her parents to speak Standard English. Keenly aware of the negative associations between Black language and intelligence in the American mainstream, Tanya's parents imposed Standard English as a required code of speech. Standard English functioned as a kind of shield to ward off any negative evaluations of her intelligence and social potential.

The problem was that, although she spoke it herself, Tanya perceived Standard English as a language of White people. In Tanya's self-perception there was a gap between the language which she spoke and the culture she loved. Tanya felt a constant vulnerability to being looked upon as White and her participation in teacher education was shaped by two factors: the struggle to maintain African American cultural integrity, and a constant cultural insecurity.

Tanya's orientation to cultural struggle emerged very clearly as she related stories about childhood interactions with her father. Tanya's father possessed an acute sensitivity to the impact of White cultural power and maintained a combative posture to the White mainstream. Tanya's accounts speak to the connection between Black self-love, childhood, and the need to fight the common sense of mainstream culture:

I think that it was important that my first dolls and toys that I liked, were carved from ebony, things like that, as opposed to white Barbie dolls. As a little child I didn't understand the significance of African carved toys, or drums. But, later in life my first image of female beauty wasn't Barbie! My father made a point of telling us when we'd watch cartoons, "Do you see any Black people on there?"

Tanya's father's sensitivity to White power directly impacted her schooling experiences:

My father didn't want us to go into the public schools, because he thought it was a tool of the government. It could brainwash you or whatever . . . [He] didn't want me exposed to that. He felt that the public school system was geared toward the White middle class. I see the value of that now. But back then I didn't.

Through the age of fourteen, Tanya was educated in exclusively African American educational settings—first in an African American independent school and then in an all-Black Catholic school. During these years, Tanya's father taught a common sense connection between African cultural awareness and the acquisition of academic skills, which Tanya referred to as "exposure":

Tanya: My father was really into reading. He was a musician. He just believed in exposure, period.
Shuaib: What do you mean by exposure?
Tanya: We were in class the other day and this girl was complaining about third graders worrying about how to spell "Chaka Zulu." But she explains that they're never going to even have to know how to spell that word. And they have it on their spelling list. And I remember when I was little, before I went to school, my father made me read. I knew how to spell that word. It was important to me because he was an African King.

Through reading at an early age and exposure to a vast array of African cultural information, Tanya developed academically and culturally at the same time. This connection between culture and academic skills enabled Tanya to reach high levels of achievement in school and possess an impressive degree of confidence in her academic abilities. It was this confidence, due in part to her father's culturally based teaching, which enabled her to interact so effectively within her teacher education classroom.

Tanya's outstanding academic performance enabled her to gain admission to a prestigious, yet predominantly White, private high school. In this setting, Tanya encountered, perhaps for the first time, African Americans who did not possess a conscious identification with Africa and African American culture. In contrast to Linda, for whom all African Americans fell into an unproblematic "Black experience," Tanya created categories for the different African Americans she encountered in high school. According to Tanya, African Americans consisted of three types: oreos, middle-class non-oreos, and lower-income. The latter two categories formed what Tanya referred to as the "African American cluster," meaning that the oreos were an outcast group that failed to even qualify as "African American."

"Oreos" were those "who decided that they were going to be as white as they could be." Tanya uses the example of language to explain what trying to be "White" means.

> There was the African American cluster, then there were what we called oreos. And those were the people who decided that they were going to be as White as they could. They changed their accent. And I can't... I've been teased because people say I talk "proper," but I don't. My accent isn't totally... umm... accent and language have a lot to do with everything I say.

In her explanation, Tanya had difficulty justifying the difference between herself and the oreos since both spoke Standard English. This revealed Tanya's own vulnerability to being an oreo, according to her own criteria. Tanya also acknowledged past experiences wherein she was teased because of the way that she spoke. This difficulty is an example of Tanya's personal struggle against the assimilating impact of White cultural power. Perhaps

Tanya's most eloquent statement about her struggle against such power occurred in her recollection of an experience as a camp counselor in a racially integrated camp setting:

> When I was working in Day-camp, I don't (hesitates) I don't think I like working in interracial settings, because the Black children or the minority group has to assimilate, it seems. I had this one little girl in camp. There were three Black children and she was the only one who didn't give up her Black culture to be more like the White girls. You know I had one other little girl, she didn't do that. She spoke just like they spoke and always around them. There was another girl who was Nigerian. Her mother was White . . . and they commented to the other girl, "You would be so much prettier if you were lighter." And that, you know . . . They were in the third grade and I just know from my own interracial school settings, those are feelings that go on, you know, giving up your culture to be with everybody else, the White girls. Those things stick with children when they grow up. Cause when I got teased and called "White," that bothered me (laughs painfully). The third grade, growing up you don't forget it. And I'm like, you know, she's not going to forget.

As in the account of her high school experiences, Tanya faces a difficult negotiation. She deeply identifies with African American culture, yet speaks in a manner which she identifies with being White. Tanya's ability to blend into the teacher education program is more problematic than appearances might indicate. Underlying her ease of interaction is a vigorous struggle to maintain her own sense of cultural integrity as a Black woman.

Language attitudes are as central to education and the teaching process as any of the skills which schools convey. The Professional School Program, the teacher education program attended by Linda and Tanya, valued Standard English as the only correct English.

The Professional School Program required that teacher candidates conform to Standard English norms in every aspect of their academic as well as professional practice. Teacher candidates were evaluated on oral language use, written essays, lesson plans, lesson materials, classroom assignments, and student handouts. Every detail had to conform to Standard English. An administrator in the program stated this requirement clearly:

> There are some things that we know from experience that they [teacher candidates] are going to have to be able to do. Time responsibilities [and] having materials prepared for children in a detailed enough fashion, that are in the standard form, standard grammar, Standard English.

This criterion clearly implies that any other form of speech is unacceptable and deficient. As we know from Linda and Tanya's African American cultural common sense, they place no such negative value upon African American English. Linda speaks African American English as her mother tongue. The very people who are most supportive of her academic achievement reinforce a way of speaking which now brings her into direct opposition to that which is acceptable within the Professional School Program.

Tanya, while speaking Standard English, not only does not see African American English as negative, but identifies it as the only legitimate speech practice of African American culture. In fact, she sees Standard English as distancing her from a full embrace of African American culture, a source of considerable personal pain. These contrasting conceptions of language deeply influence Linda and Tanya's experience in teacher education.

Due to the protective quality of her life within the "Black Experience," Linda saw nothing wrong with the way that she spoke. Linda's first awareness of the mainstream's judgment of her speech occurred in an evaluation conference with her public school teacher mentor:

> *Linda:* I think my [cooperating] teacher mentioned it to me during one of our [evaluative] conferences . . . You can tell

she didn't want to bring it up, but she did. And she was like, "I notice that you had said 'had did.' " And she started trying to quiz me on the verb participles and stuff. And you know I was like, "I don't know all the rules, you know. I mean I forgot some of 'em. I mean but I got my little book if you want me to bring it out. But I know what I'm supposed to say." I said I probably said that. But when they said it again, they said it in conference. And I noticed that on each of my evaluations that they had whitened it out and put me a point lower on that aspect of oral talk.

Following the evaluation, Linda became intensely aware, not only of her own speech, but also of the speech of everyone around her. The initial target of her new awareness of language was her family and her community peers because she realized that her difficulties were the result of her speaking as they did. She began to associate her family, those most responsible for her educational success, with her academic difficulties.

But what I'm sayin is that everybody around us speaks it. How can we get rooted out of it when I, like I say, when I just be observin. I notice my mother gets it. Sometimes she would say "does," sometimes she would say "he do, she do." I notice all my friends would say it. I mean everybody that's any Black person that I was around would say that same thing . . . And how could you change it if you constantly around the same people everyday using the same messed up words.

"Messed up words," demonstrates how Linda began to internalize the "common sense" of the White mainstream, the judgment that Black language is "messed up." Not only did she start to internalize this set of language values, but she applied them to the speech of her family and friends. Not only did Linda begin to see herself as flawed, but she saw her entire community speaking a language that needed to be rooted out.

The evaluation and the very explicit manner in which the quality of Linda's speech was literally "whited out," demonstrates how an external power can force a change in self-perception. Although such evaluations aspire to be objective, and are considered technical and impersonal, Linda experienced this one as extremely personal. Asa Hilliard suggests that these kinds of objective and technical evaluations hold the potential for making African American students feel ashamed and hopeless.

One tenet of the mainstream common sense about African American English is that its users are less intelligent than individuals who speak Standard English. Linguists such as John Baugh have found that many in the teaching profession hold similar attitudes and believe that those speakers of African American English are less capable of expressing ideas in an academic manner. Linda encountered these beliefs about her academic possibilities when she found the following statement written on a typewritten assignment: "Did you write these passages? It doesn't look like your writing. Please give references." Linda kept drafts of her work and was cleared of the suspicion of plagiarism, however, Linda regarded the comment as an indictment against her intelligence and academic potential. Mainstream common sense suggests that if Linda speaks African American English, then she cannot possibly perform at an acceptable academic level. The professor's common sense left Linda disoriented and confused, not knowing whether to view the comment as an indirect compliment on the quality of her work or an insult:

And why just be that blunt and say, "Did you write these?" You know, "Give references." And I'm glad that they think it came out of another book. That makes me feel good, really that they questioned it. But that just looks ... What do they think of me, then?

Regardless of the reason for the comments, it is clear that the writer holds inaccurate conceptions regarding the academic performance possibilities of speakers of African American English. Linda later observed that the writer could have expected her writing to contain African American English and when it was not evident, assumed that the Standard English writing had to have been plagiarized. Writing, however, offers much more moment-to-moment control in the communication process. Students who have difficulty speaking Standard English can more successfully write it because they can be more conscious of editing their communication.

Through teacher professional preparation, Linda's language and speech were judged as flawed. Because she spoke African American English, Linda had two of the most profound experiences of personal and cultural devaluation that one could imagine within an academic setting. Not only was her intelligence called into question, but her personal and academic integrity as well.

In contrast to Linda, Tanya was prepared for cultural conflict and struggle. Her mother had just recently completed her own teacher education program and warned Tanya about the academic dangers of failing to speak Standard English:

> My mother told me that "They're probably going to pick on you because you're Black and how you talk." Because she was saying that they did that to her when she was student teaching. So she told me that I would have to be careful and be sure to speak like they speak because they're going to pick on that.

One might assume that because she spoke Standard English, Tanya would not experience language problems. However, despite her speech, Tanya was still subject to the mainstream "common sense" perception that, as an African American, she was supposed to be deficient. At one of her practical experience placements, a substitute teacher had been assigned to replace the regular teacher in the classroom where Tanya was assigned. During the course of the day, the substitute lost control of the class. Seeing the problem and the potential for chaos, Tanya stepped in and restored order and learning. After the incident in which she outperformed the White substitute, Tanya remembers the substitute making the following comments.

She started saying well, she said something to the effect of "Don't be offended, I might use the wrong words," but she said, "You don't act like you're Black." And I knew what she meant by it. So I wasn't offended . . . But I guess she was referring to my dialect.

As Tanya had proven to be professionally competent, even more competent than the substitute, Tanya could no longer remain "Black" in the substitute teacher's mind. In mainstream common sense, being Black is associated with incompetence, bad English, and general inferiority to White performance.

Tanya's claim of not being offended by the substitute's remark was not entirely accurate. As one might imagine, it touched deeply held insecurities, even anger, about her inability to be viewed as African American. Later, in a journal entry about the incident, Tanya provided a different picture of the impact of the substitute teacher's remark:

She'd never been saved by an African American before. She also told me that I didn't act like I was Black. That hurts. I am not White. I don't want to be White or denied any relation to my culture. I don't feel I should be defined as a person by European American culture. This society is very frustrating to me.

Throughout African American history, a clash between African American common sense and the common sense of the White mainstream produces a new common sense—the sense of "playing the game." Playing the game implies an awareness that many different types of common sense exist simultaneously, with some having more power than others. Depending upon one's needs, one must conform to the common sense in power at that moment. For Linda and Tanya, mainstream common sense had the power to determine whether or not they would be able to become teachers. Amidst the clash of common senses which marked their experiences as teacher candidates, Linda and Tanya learned how to play the game.

When she received a negative evaluation because of the way she spoke, Linda first questioned herself, her family, and her community. Eventually, however, Linda turned the same awareness of language toward the teacher education program and its enforcement of language rules. She observed the language practices of those around her and saw that, while others used non-Standard English, their practices went unnoticed. She began to see that the rules of language were very complicated. Negative evaluations depended upon the form of non-Standard English used, and who used it.

> Cause I notice like White people, they say "anyways." And it's not supposed to be "anyways." But they never correct them on that, and they're so busy looking for us, and they miss that. You know. So why not correct them on "anyways"? And they say some things wrong themselves which, you know, I guess it's OK if they said it, or if they don't realize it, cause they're so busy always trying to look out for us.

Linda also found the speech of an African American cooperating teacher to whom she was assigned similar to her own.

> And I told you, ever since that incident, I've just been noticing how Black people talk. My "cooperating" teacher is Black now. She done said "had did," "she do," and not using the right verbs. And I notice that she do it all the time. So I'm like when I get back to the suggestion that I go to the writing lab to learn how to talk or whatever, I'm like should I ask whether my co-op should go with me because she say the same things I do?

Noticing the inconsistent application of rules regarding the use of non-Standard English in the Professional School Program ena-

bled Linda to deflect the burden of the Program's negative evaluation of her oral speech. By identifying these inconsistencies, she
was able to realize that common sense conceptions of language
standards are really no measure of intelligence or academic potential. Instead, she saw that the language rules are part of a game,
a game in which who you are and the position you hold weighs
heavily on how language "standards" are applied.

Eventually, Linda began to integrate this understanding of the
game into her teaching identity. When I asked Linda to speculate
regarding how she would help her future students based upon her
experiences as a teacher candidate, her response demonstrated how
she had moved beyond the womb of cultural protection and into
the game of cultural struggle.

> [I'll tell them] you gonna be labeled as just a little dumb
> thug who can't do nothing. You know, it's all right to wear
> your earring, it's all right to wear your baseball hat. But you
> know, you just have to know, you have to prove them wrong.
> You have to work harder, just because you're Black. You
> might be smarter than Suzie, but you gonna work. You gonna
> work twice as hard as Suzie. That's just the way it is, and I
> don't know when it's gonna change. I don't know if it's gonna
> change. But that's what you gotta do.

Given the manner in which she had been victimized by language beliefs, Tanya began to use her culturally based academic
confidence to question the beliefs within which she had been
trapped. Specifically, Tanya conducted personal research into the
nature and origins of African American English in order to make
arguments in Standard English against demands for the exclusive
use of Standard English. Tanya developed a very sophisticated understanding of the historical emergence of African American English, and the difficulties associated with learning it. These
historical factors helped Tanya to dispute the myth that African
American English reflects an intelligence flaw and make the case
that this perception is a function of White economic and political

power. Tanya even used her insights to support Linda during her difficulties:

> *Linda:* So when you say "dialect," you're talking about specific words, phrases, and the tone.
>
> *Tanya:* I'm talkin about the whole.... There are grammatical patterns. In Black dialect, "had did" is a grammatical pattern. If you trace back to the languages we spoke before were taken over here as slaves, you can compare black vernacular English with these languages and see that there's a connecting pattern.
>
> *Linda:* Really?
>
> *Tanya:* Yeah.... It was hard for them to learn English. Nobody sat down and gave Black people English classes. We just worked the field. So you know we weren't given these superior English classes when slavery ended either. So that's what we picked up, a second language the best way we could. And we made it a dialect, and that's what happened. And that's just what happened. A lot of White people have had to do the same thing.

Tanya also celebrated the knowledge required of African Americans to become "bilingual" and criticized the Professional School Program for not recognizing these strengths:

> *Tanya:* But you have to think of it this way. They're not commending you on being bilingual. And the ability to switch back and forth is being bilingual. And by telling you that you're wrong and you need help as opposed to modeling Standard English, they're not modeling these wonderful teaching strategies that they want us to use. And it's wrong for them to sit up there and say that "you talk wrong" or what have you. What they could do is say, "There's non-Standard English and there's modern Standard English and we would prefer for you to use Standard English. If you need help speaking Standard English, then we can go over that." But

they are out of line to tell you that you speak incorrectly and that you need help. That's unprofessional and what's the use of reading all these articles or having us read them if they don't fully understand them.

As with Linda, Tanya's critical insights helped her to clearly see the game-like quality of mainstream common sense language beliefs. Mainstream common sense, like the teaching profession, is meant to perpetuate the well-being of the culture in power. Yet, as this culture has economic and political power, strategic accommodations must be made. The teaching program sees "difference," denigrates it, and tries to correct it. It's blind to any other common sense which may be academically and linguistically valid. Tanya, in her ability to identify the cultural blindness of the teaching profession and its language ideology, came to the important realization that she needed to go beyond its instruction and create her own standards:

> In terms of this experience, I have to look at it as, they're gonna have their own criteria. You're always gonna have somebody, if you're going to be a teacher the rest of your life, somebody bossing you around. So you gotta get your own level of self confidence together, and set criteria for yourself. And I think at the beginning of the year, I guess if I had all the assignments and gotten certain [low] grades it would have hurt me more. But now I don't care, because I figure I'm smart enough to do it if I want to. And I have to structure my own style. . . . And knowing when I have to put up a front. . . . Knowing what it calls for, cause it's in their game. . . . And I think it's good when you can create your own style. You can help other people to see the structure [of the game], and work within it and create their own style.

Within the teaching profession, both Linda and Tanya faced significant challenges to maintain the self-esteem and cultural integrity which they brought to the task of teaching. Linda's exposure to the direct manner in which her language was devalued led her to look negatively, not only upon herself, but upon her family and community as well. During her preparation for the teaching profession, Linda's intelligence, academic potential, and even her personal integrity were called into question. Linda's experiences were a direct result of the mainstream common sense conception that a speaker of African American English is not capable of doing quality work.

Tanya, who spoke Standard English, faced a different challenge. Her esteem and cultural self-love were challenged by the deep-seated insecurity she felt because she conformed to mainstream language requirements. During her preparation to become a teacher, Tanya's insecurity and frustration were made worse by the mainstream language beliefs in the teaching profession. While Linda, as a speaker of African American English, could not be intelligent and academically competent, Tanya faced the mainstream perception that she could not be professionally competent, be a speaker of Standard English, and still be Black.

However, in spite of the attacks against their personal and cultural integrity, Linda and Tanya, often through conversation with one another, developed an important survival insight. They realized, in different ways, that mainstream common sense, although pervasive and powerful, is not *truth*. Once they were able to see and question mainstream common sense, Linda and Tanya cultivated an alternative common sense of "the game." The game is about maintaining appearances but, most of all, it is about maintaining the confidence to defy the official institutional messages and to construct one's own standards, standards rooted in cultural and experiential common sense and the same Black self-love which enabled them to achieve academically in the first place.

CHAPTER 12

"We don't talk right. You ask him."

JOAN WYNNE

After witnessing bright young students and concerned parents who stopped themselves from speaking publicly because they "don't talk right," educator JOAN WYNNE explored the pervasive myth of language supremacy held by students, teachers-in-training, and in-service teachers. She found that the concept of Standard English as correct, neutral, and universal is nurtured in the classroom, where it is almost always the only dialect used and accepted. First, Wynne urges, it is imperative that teachers are educated to understand that language validity is based on politics, not science; only then can they understand how the exclusive endorsement of one dialect is a disservice to all children, not only children of color. Instilling in our children respect for and familiarity with other dialects would allow them to construe a truer version of American history, be fuller human beings for having access to multiple expressions of reality, and be better prepared to deal with the complexities of a shifting, shrinking world.

The world is richer than it is possible to express in any single language.

—ILYA PRIGOGINE

It was over twenty years ago, but it could have happened yesterday. I had taken a group of African American high school newspaper staff to a university journalism workshop and awards ceremony. There were about eight students with me that day to learn more about print journalism, and, more importantly, to receive an award for one of the ten best high school newspapers in the metropolitan area.

We were sitting together, in a sea of White faces, listening to one of the media experts talk about ways to improve school newspapers. After he had spoken, he opened the session to questions. My students had several they wanted to ask in their effort to discover new ways of writing creatively for their peers back at school. One of my editors leaned over to me and whispered, "Here is a list of questions we want you to ask him."

I said, "No, you ask him," surprised that my student and his cohort were suddenly shy.

"We don't talk right. You ask him."

No amount of encouragement from me would prompt them to speak. What I now know is that until that moment, I did not understand how psychologically damaging language biases are. I watched eight students, who happened to be some of the brightest young people I have ever taught, shrink from their brilliance. Here they sat, knowing they had competed with other journalism staffs for the best newspaper—and won—yet, at the same time, they felt inferior. They were silenced by language biases born of racism, biases that crippled their inquisitive natures. Their typical bold acts of discovery became impotent in the midst of a White majority. And the majority lost a golden opportunity to hear my students' thoughts and learn from their brilliance.

Looking back now, I recognize the full measure of my own miseducation. My schooling had not prepared me, as an English major, to understand the depth and breadth of language oppression. No one had taught me that the language I had grown up loving was used to bludgeon others into submission and feelings of inferiority. But even worse none of my teachers had ever encouraged me to assist these youngsters in creating a psychological sanctuary so they didn't succumb to unfounded language bias when exposed to the dominant culture. In the absence of that instruction, I had made those adolescents vulnerable to the prejudices of the majority, reflected in their own internalized notions of being linguistically inadequate. Nothing had prepared my students or me for that moment of defeat, a moment when they should have been reveling in victorious celebration.

Many years later, during a trip to South Africa, I was once more made aware of the contradictions in perceptions of language between a dominant culture and the "other." While helping to build houses in Alexandria, a black township outside of Johannesburg, I consistently heard from White South Africans how deficient Black South Africans were in their use of language, how they were slow in thinking, and how much "like children" they were. In fact, almost every complaint reminded me of the remarks describing American Blacks that I had heard while growing up in the South. Again, though, those remarks were in conflict with the reality that presented itself to me as I worked in Alexandria. I was often surrounded by young children attempting to help in our construction efforts. Their warmth and friendliness always charmed me, but it was their language facility that totally disarmed me. Those small children, four, five, six, and seven years old, easily moved from speaking Swahili to Xhosa to English to Afrikaans to Zulu, and several other languages that I can't even remember the names of now. In that small two-mile radius of a township, where over two million people from many different cultures were herded together by the rules of apartheid, Black children had quickly learned to communicate across the cultural divides. Amazingly, though, despite that gift of language facility, the same insidious myths about language superiority ran rampant. And the myths are destructive. They lie about people's ability to think, and, perhaps, equally as tragic, they prevent the dominant culture from learning from the gifts of "the other."

Sometimes, the lie seems to take on a life of its own. At Morehouse College, the United States' premier African American male college, where I taught for fourteen years, I observed intelligent, sophisticated students misled by those myths. There, young men parroted what they had heard mainstream English teachers, like myself, proclaim for years, that the use of standard English was "talking right." In Morehouse classrooms, the students and I would often struggle through discussions on the speech patterns of the children who lived in the housing projects surrounding the college and who were mentored by the Morehouse students. My college students often would argue with me about my contention that the language of those children was as valid as theirs. Because the Morehouse students had fallen prey to invalidated linguistic assumptions of the mainstream culture, they had no tolerance for the speech of these children. The mentors assumed that the children's speech indicated not only linguistic, but cognitive deficit. Of course, if we want these children to be socially and economically mobile in mainstream culture, we must teach them standard English; yet, if we reject them by rejecting the language they grew up with, we alienate them from the very places where they could learn the standard dialect. And by teaching children that their language is inferior, we teach a lie.

The lasting impact of that lie became clear again only last week at a town meeting of parents in a small Southern school district where approximately three to four hundred middle- and upper-middle-class mainstream parents and working-class African American parents met to discuss possible changes in their elementary

schools. Out of the twenty or so parents who spoke at the micro-
phone, only one was an African American parent. After the meeting I was told by several of the African American mothers that
while they felt very strongly about the issues at stake, they could
not and would not speak to the whole group because they felt
uncomfortable about their speech in front of those mainstream
parents. They had no trouble articulating their ideas to me, but
only after I had approached them asking why they had chosen to
remain silent. Like my former journalism staff, those parents harbored the mistaken notion that their speech was not good enough
to air in front of a majority White audience. Yes, the distortions
we teach in schools last a long time. In those places we begin to
hush the voices that might lead the way out of the labyrinth of
our educational malpractices. That silencing "like a cancer grows"
(Simon and Garfunkel, 1966).

Teaching language supremacy
distorts reality for mainstream children

I believe that the abuses of linguistic oppression toward the children of color are horrendous; the consequences are severe; and the
damage to the self-esteem of youths is unconscionable. But, I also
believe that there is another dark side to this issue—the severe
consequences of notions of language supremacy for the children of
the dominant culture.

By neglecting to teach about the beauty and richness of the
language of Black America, we also damage White children. If we
believe as James Baldwin that all languages define, articulate, and
reveal individual realities ("Black English," 1997), then by not
recognizing Ebonics, we keep white children trapped in myopic
visions of world realities. We give them one more reason to bolster
their mistaken notions of supremacy and privilege. If we believe,
too, as Baldwin suggests, that Black English "is rooted in American
history," then, by discounting Ebonics, we keep White children
oblivious to significant slices of their own country's history. We

deny them the opportunity to look at their own ancestors and history in a way that might help them recognize their collective responsibility for injustices, as well as their collective potential for redemption.

In a nation that is home to a multitude of cultures, and in a world that, through technology, has become a global village, cross-cultural respect and understanding are imperative. Yet if our main-stream children think that their language is superior to others, how can they expect anyone else to believe that they, the privileged, value other people's cultures? With such notions, how will our children ever work collaboratively across cultures to build those bridges of understanding that will allow people to cross the racial divide that separates us as a nation, a world, and a species?

We have learned that prejudice of any kind can stifle our chil-dren's growth in critical thinking. In *The Open and Closed Mind* (1960), M. Rokeach found that:

> Persons who are high in ethnic prejudice and/or authoritar-ianism, as compared with persons who are low, are more rigid in their problem-solving behavior, more concrete in their thinking, and more narrow in their grasp of a particular sub-ject; they also have a greater tendency to premature closure in their perceptual processes and to distortions in memory, and a greater tendency to be intolerant of ambiguity (p. 16).

As Rokeach suggests, by fostering prejudice such as language biases, we stifle all students' cognitive development. Thinking their language is a superior language, which is, after all, what too many teachers teach and too many in society believe, White children may become incapable of really hearing other cultures and, thus, learning from them (Allport, 1958; Hall, 1989). For as long as mainstream students think that another's language is inferior to theirs, they will probably not bother to understand it, and there-fore, there will be much about the other that they will always fail to understand. Not only will this further widen the cultural di-vide, but it will prevent the group in power from accessing the knowledge base—and, subsequently, potential solutions to a myriad of world problems—of those deemed "other" by virtue of language form.

Several weeks ago one of my university colleagues explained to me that she had recently tried to listen to a noted African American historian who, during a television interview, continuously referred to every Black person he spoke about as "Brother" or "Sister." This cultural tradition seemed excessive to my associate, annoying her to the point that she felt forced to switch the channel. The seemingly intrusive nature of this different linguistic ritual kept her from hearing the message of a nationally respected scholar of history. For her, and I think for too many of us, our obsession with the familiar form can obliterate the significance of the content. I have found in my thirty years of experience in the education profession that this kind of unconscious intolerance of difference cuts us off from learning from one another.

My colleague was so uncomfortable with a cultural pattern of speech that it forced her to "tune out" a speaker whom she knew to be a reputable scholar. Might her reaction suggest the serious intellectual consequences of intolerance, cited earlier in Rokeach's study—that if cultural intolerance is strong, it is more difficult to take in new information? Except for those with telepathic gifts, language is the closest way humans know of getting inside another person's head. If our tolerance of language diversity is so fragile that we turn away from those persons who exhibit cultural linguistic patterns different from ours, how can we ever expect to begin to understand each other and, thereby, build a community of learners? If the tolerance is that fragile, how can those of us who are responsible for educating the next generation of teachers adequately teach them to be sensitive to the language differences of the children they teach or of other faculty members with whom they work?

Language supremacy and the education of teachers

Recently, I gave a short questionnaire to fifteen pre-service teachers at a university asking them their opinions about Ebonics and Standard English. These students are in their last months of their undergraduate program. Because they were not new to the university nor to teacher training, I was surprised at some of their responses. Most of the students responded to the question, "How would you describe 'Standard English'?" with the answer, "Correct English," or "Proper English." When answering questions about the description and use of Ebonics, one intern said, "To me, ebonics is the use of incorrect english. . . . I do not think that allowing children to speak 'ebonics' in the classroom does them a service. I think that 'standard English' is the grammatically correct form of the English language." His response typified the answers of the others in the group.

One student response, however, seemed more emotional and dogmatic than the others. "Ebonics," she said, "should not be allowed in the classroom. Our education system should not cater to lower standards of language." She and a few of the other soon-to-be teachers were unknowingly expressing one of the basic tenets of linguistics: that languages are defined politically, not scientifically—and that a "language is a dialect with an army and a navy" (Dorsett, 1997, O'Neil, 1997). The responses of the pre-service teachers reflected no awareness that each dialect and language has an internal integrity unto itself; that one language clearly is not scientifically better than the other, but that one is politically more acceptable than the other—for one dialect belongs to the power structure (Dorsett, 1997; Fillmore 1998; Perry and Delpit, 1998).

As I continued to read the comments of these university students, I wondered why, when language is the major medium of instruction, would we in schools of education give so little time, effort, and attention to teaching our pre-service teachers about the basic assumptions of the realities of language diversity? Why would we choose to ignore the significance of instructing all of our interns, whether they are to teach mathematics, science, language arts, or shop, that language is a political decision and a group experience of a lived reality, not a manifestation of intellectual prowess or language superiority?

In the same semester, in another course of thirty-four graduate students, most of whom are practicing teachers, I listened to a class discussion about African American children's language. This very heated debate emerged from discussing the question, "What is excellence in urban education?" During the discussion, none of the students addressed the political nature of selecting one dialect as the "standard dialect." The one thing that all participants seemed to agree upon was that all students needed to know "proper" or "correct" English. Many insisted that anytime a student used Ebonics in the classroom, she should be corrected. How is it that we might forget to inform every pre-service and in-service student that all teachers are obliged to honor the many languages we speak? As James Baldwin, Toni Morrison, and many others suggest, language is who we are. If any of us refuse to respect the other's language, it becomes too easy, consciously or unconsciously, to then disrespect the person.

Later, I gave a language attitude questionnaire to five teachers, who were asked to give them to their individual faculties. With very few exceptions, the teachers' responses reflected the same assumptions about Ebonics and "Standard English" as the university pre-service and graduate students. One teacher answered that Ebonics should never be spoken in the classroom because "it sounds ridiculous and illiterate." Without an apparent understanding of multilingualism in any form, another teacher said all children should speak "Standard English" because, "We are a part of the Human Race and Standard English is the common denominator," adding that Standard English was a "neutral and universal language." Even those teachers who voiced some respect for Ebonics speakers agreed that children should not speak Ebonics in the classroom. With the research that is now available about the importance of schools accepting a child's home language while still teaching them the standard dialect, too many teachers are astoundingly ignorant of the basic truths about language. The lack of knowledge about language development amongst many of our teachers spoke to a gap in the professional development of these teachers; and, to me, it suggests as well how insignificant many colleges of education may assume that kind of knowledge is.

But such neglect by colleges to include in their curriculum the politics of language is no small matter. Growing up in a segregated South, I saw "up close and personal" the impact of that neglect on the psyches of children. The ignorance of teachers, myself included, about the role of institutional power in deciding whose language is "standard" played a part in making many African American children feel inferior about their home language when they were in school. Moreover, all children—as well as teachers—who are never given a forum to examine the oppressive assumption that one language is better than another become vulnerable to other acts of oppression. It is an egregious failure for colleges to cavalierly omit from teacher-education any discussions of the political ramifications of language use and acceptance. Teachers without this knowledge will limit the worlds of White children and make children of other ethnicities vulnerable to the negative views held by educators and society in general regarding their cognitive competence.

Again, none of this discussion is to suggest that the Standard Dialect is not to be taught to our students from kindergarten through college—it is, after all, the language of power, the chosen form of communication of those who own the missiles, the tanks, the banks, the bombs, and the government. But its importance as a *dialect* must be put in a context that produces less damage to ourselves and our students. Glorifying Standard English as a superior mode of expression is intellectually limiting.

What should happen in classrooms?

Nothing short of a revolution in our language instruction will suffice. Mainstream children and children of color suffer from their linguistic "mis-education." Ironically, we in the dominant culture do not seem to recognize the contradictions in our attitudes about the language Black people use. We are fascinated with the cleverness of Ebonics, as shown by our incorporation of many of its idioms into our everyday speech. For example, mainstream television personalities such as the *Today* show's Katie Couric and Matt Lauer have consistently used such phrases as "Don't 'diss' me like that" and "my bad" during their morning banter. Mainstream advertisers, too, often use expressions and rhythms from rap music to sell their products. Yet at the same time, most of our media and educational institutions insist that the language is somehow inferior to the Standard Dialect. Perhaps, we might share those kinds of contradictions with our students as a way to begin our conversations about the political nature of language choice.

The brilliant writing of Nobel Prize–winning author Toni Morrison might be a great starting place for yeasty discussions on the merits of diverse languages and dialects, of issues of racism, and of the power of storytelling to connect us to our individual and collective history. We can use her words to teach African American children the majesty of their home languages, and White children the beauty and validity of other languages. Morrison explains that language "is the thing that black people love so much—the saying of words, holding them on the tongue, experimenting with them, playing with them. It's a love, a passion." By saying this she suggests a very different relationship between her people and their language from that portrayed anywhere in the mainstream culture. It's a perspective that pre-service and in-service teachers might explore to counteract the erroneous messages that academia, the media, and other institutions send us about the inferior "dialect" of African Americans.

Linguist Charles Fillmore, in a speech delivered at UC Berkeley, suggested that educators might "offer serious units in dialect in middle school and high school classes throughout the country as a general part of language education" for all children (Fillmore 1998). Walt Wolfram, another noted linguistic scholar, suggested that activities in such units make it possible for children to "discover generalizations and systematicities in their own speech and in the speech of others" (Fillmore 1998).

Recently, hearing "the speech of others" caused a visceral reawakening in me of the power of language diversity. While attending Al Sharpton's "Shadow Inauguration" rally in Washington, D.C., I heard a dozen or more African American speakers give testimony to the part they, their parents, or their grandparents had played in turning a nation around. They spoke of shattering notions of segregated equality; of dismantling unfair voting laws; and of surviving as a people killings, lynching, attacks by dogs and by police wielding billy clubs and water hoses. While listening to these stories, I thought about the Southern Freedom movement and of its impact on freedom movements in China, in South Africa, and other parts of the globe (Harding, 1999). I remembered that representatives of only 13 percent of the population of the United States forever changed the South, the nation, and the world. That day I stood in the midst of throngs of descendents of Africans as they chanted "No Justice, No Peace"; as they sang "Ain't gonna' let nobody turn me 'round"; and "a walkin'...a talkin'...Marching up to freedom land." The power of the words, of the rhythm, of the cadences of the slogans moved me as we marched in the rain toward the Supreme Court Building to register our disapproval of its justices' most recent decision against voting rights.

I came home with those chants, those testimonies, ringing in my ears. And I couldn't help but wonder.... How dare we patronize as an inferior dialect the language of such heroes and sheroes? Those now grown-up activists who created the sit-ins of the '60s, who walked in the marches, who survived the jails, have told me about the power of the chants, the songs, the language to keep them alive, committed, and unified in a struggle that no one thought they could win (Conversations, 1988, 2000, 2001; Reagon, 1998; King, 1987). That language and those stories belong in our children's classrooms.

Joseph Campbell, in *The Hero with a Thousand Faces* (1968), tells us that a hero must assimilate his opposite, must put aside his pride, and in the end must realize "that he and his opposite are not of differing species, but one flesh." We have to educate our White children to understand that we are, indeed, "one flesh." That we are "the other." Then, what a gift to teach them that they are connected to the heroism of those African American students who engaged in sit-ins and marches; who against all odds survived arrests and beatings; and who created "a dazzling moment of clarity" for the South and the nation (Curry 2000). To be taught that they belong not only to the history of the oppressor but also to the history of those who so bravely fought and won those battles for justice is a lesson all children deserve to hear.

What a breath of fresh air it would be for our young people to read about other young people who nonviolently took on a violent and corrupt government and won. To use their language and their stories in the classroom might be one of the greatest lessons of empowerment we could give all of America's children. Telling our students of the audacity of ordinary young people like themselves, who dared to think they had the right to shape the world around them, might do more toward creating critical thinkers in our classrooms than any of the other pedagogical tricks that we have up our sleeves.

Alice Walker, in *The Same River Twice: Honoring the Difficult* (1996), says that "even to attempt to respectfully encounter 'the other' is a sacred act, and leads to and through the labyrinth. To the river. Possibly to healing. A 'special effect' of the soul." Encountering the other is difficult, for all humans, whether it be in language or in ritual; yet, for me, it sometimes seems the only way we will ever make this democracy work. If we in schools of education stay silent while others proclaim language superiority, how do we help our students "respectfully encounter 'the other' "? Shouldn't we, who teach teachers, create spaces in our classrooms to explore the political nature of language choices? Shouldn't we in our courses facilitate discussions about the need to value diverse languages, especially in these rocky political times? That we are sending into public school classrooms, teachers whose limited knowledge about language caused them to respond so dismally to a questionnaire about Ebonics suggests that we are failing our teachers' intellectual development, failing their future students' language growth, and failing our troubled democracy. Helping students, in a fragmented modern society, make connections to each other and to a larger world is a respectable outcome (Delpit 1997; Hilliard 1997; Palmer 1998; Wilson 1998) that many scholars believe can be advanced through the study of diverse dialects and languages. Learning the skills of reading, writing, and mathematics, as well as every other discipline, can happen within that context of making connections.

As they learn those skills, our students need a time and space to discover that the interdependence of all of humanity and of all species is a concept that poets and mystics have proclaimed for thousands of years, and is now one that physicists are validating through their study of the universe, from the subatomic level to the formation of the galaxies. Our students need to understand that scientists are continuously discovering the complex interconnectedness of all life, matter, and energy. And all students need to learn that notions of supremacy, whether they come in the shape of superior races or superior languages, do not fit into that grand scheme of things (Bogardus 1960). Finally, all of us need to remind ourselves of what Ilya Prigogine's quotation at the head of this chapter seems to suggest—that the worship of a single language limits our ability to know and to express that interconnectedness, that "full richness of the world."

REFERENCES

Allport, G. W. (1958). *The Nature of Prejudice.* Garden City, NY: Doubleday.

Baldwin, James (1997). "If Black English Isn't a Language, Then Tell Me, What Is?" *Rethinking Schools,* Fall, Vol. 12, No. 1.

Bogardus, E. S. (1960). *The Development of Social Thought.* New York: Longmans, Green.

Campbell, J. (1968). 2nd ed. *Hero with a Thousand Faces.* Princeton: Princeton University Press.

Conversations with Joan Browning, February 2001.

Conversations with Connie Curry, January 1988; February 2000; February 2001.

Conversations with Charlie Cobb, Zaharah Simmons, April 2000.

Curry, Browning, et al. (2000). *Deep in Our Hearts: Nine White Women in the Freedom Movement.* Athens, GA: University of Georgia Press.

Delpit, Lisa (1997). "Ten Factors for Teaching Excellence in Urban Schools." Speech at Urban Atlanta Coalition Compact Town Meeting, September, Atlanta, GA.

Dorsett, C. (1997). *Ebonics—21st Century Racism?* Website: http://members.tripod.com/~cdorsett/ebonics.htm

Fillmore, C. (1998). Speech at UC Berkeley, http://www.cal.org/ebonics/fillmore.html

Hall, E. (1989). *Beyond Culture.* New York: Doubleday Dell, Anchor Books edition.

Hilliard, A. G. III (1997). *SBA: The Reawakening of the African Mind.* Gainesville, Fla.: Makare Publishing Co.

King, Mary (1987). *Freedom Song: A Personal Story of the 1960s Civil Rights Movement.* New York: Morrow.

Linguistic Society of America (1997). "Resolution on the Oakland 'Ebonics' Issue," http://www.lsadc.org/ebonics.html

O'Neil, Wayne (1997). "If Ebonics Isn't a Language, Then Tell Me, What Is?" *Rethinking Schools*, Fall, Vol. 12, No. 1.

Palmer, P. (1998). *The Courage to Teach.* United States: Jossey-Bass.

Perry, T., and L. Delpit (1998). *Rethinking Schools.* Boston: Beacon.

Reagon, B. J. (1998). " 'Oh Freedom': Music of the Movement," *A Circle of Trust: Remembering SNCC.* Greenberg, G., ed. New Brunswick: Rutgers University Press.

Rokeach, M. (1960). *The Open and Closed Mind.* New York: Basic Books.

Simon and Garfunkel (1966). "The Sounds of Silence." On *Sounds of Silence.* Columbia 9269.

Skutnabb-Kangas, Tove (2000). *Linguistic Genocide in Education—or Worldwide Diversity and Human Rights*. Mahwah, NJ: L. Erlbaum Associates.

Smith, Ernie A. (1976). *A Case for Bilingual and Bicultural Education for United States Slave Descendents of African Origin*. Fullerton: Department of Linguistics Seminar Series, California State University, Fullerton.

Smitherman, Geneva (1997). "Black English/Ebonics: What It Be Like?" *Rethinking Schools*, Fall, Vol. 12, No. 1.

——— (1977). *Talkin and Testifyin: The Language of Black America*. Boston: Houghton Mifflin.

Walker, Alice (1996). *The Same River Twice: Honoring the Difficult*. New York: Scribner.

Wilson, Amos (1998). *Blueprint for Black Power: A Moral, Political and Economic Imperative for the Twenty-first Century*. New York: Afrikan World InfoSystems.

Appendix:
Linguistic Society of America Resolution on the Oakland "Ebonics" Issue

Whereas there has been a great deal of discussion in the media and among the American public about the 18 December 1996 decision of the Oakland School Board to recognize the language variety spoken by many African American students and to take it into account in teaching Standard English, the Linguistic Society of America, as a society of scholars engaged in the scientific study of language, hereby resolves to make it known that:

a. The variety known as "Ebonics," "African American Vernacular English" (AAVE), and "Vernacular Black English" and by other names is systematic and rule-governed like all natural speech varieties. In fact, all human linguistic systems—spoken, signed, and written—are fundamentally regular. The systematic and expressive nature of the grammar and pronunciation patterns of the African American vernacular has been established by numerous scientific studies over the past thirty years. Characterizations of Ebonics as "slang," "mutant," "lazy," "defective," "ungrammatical," or "broken English" are incorrect and demeaning.

b. The distinction between "languages" and "dialects" is usually made more on social and political grounds than on purely linguistic ones. For example, different varieties of Chinese are popularly regarded as "dialects," though their speakers cannot understand each other, but speakers of Swedish and Norwegian, which are regarded as separate "languages," generally understand each other. What is important from a linguistic and educational point of view is not whether AAVE is called a "language" or a "dialect" but rather that its systematicity be recognized.

c. As affirmed in the LSA Statement of Language Rights (June 1996), there are individual and group benefits to maintaining vernacular speech varieties and there are scientific and human advantages to linguistic diversity. For those living in the United States there are also benefits in acquiring Standard English and resources should be made available to all who aspire to mastery of Standard English. The Oakland School Board's commitment to helping students master Standard English is commendable.

d. There is evidence from Sweden, the U.S., and other countries that speakers of other varieties can be aided in their learning of the standard variety by pedagogical approaches which recognize the legitimacy of the other varieties of a language. From this perspective, the Oakland School Board's decision to recognize the vernacular of African American students in teaching them Standard English is linguistically and pedagogically sound.

Chicago, Illinois
January 1997

SELECTED REFERENCES
(BOOKS ONLY)

Baratz, Joan C., and Roger W. Shuy, eds. (1969). Teaching Black Children to read. Washington, D.C.: Center for Applied Linguistics.

Baugh, John (1983). Black street speech: Its history, structure and survival. Austin: University of Texas Press.

Bloome, David, and J. Lemke, eds. (1995). Special Issue: Africanized English and Education. Linguistics and Education 7.

Burling, Robbins (1973). English in black and white. New York: Holt.

Butters, Ron (1989). The death of Black English: Convergence and divergence in American English. Frankfurt, Germany: Peter Lang.

Dandy, Evelyn (1991). Black communications: Breaking down the barriers. Chicago: African American Images.

DeStephano, Johanna, ed. (1973). Language, society and education: A profile of Black English. Worthington, OH: Charles A. Jones.

Dillard, J. L. (1972). Black English: Its history and usage in the United States. New York: Random House.

Fasold, Ralph W., and Roger W. Shuy, eds. (1970). Teaching Standard English in the inner city. Washington, D.C.: Center of Applied Linguistics.

Gadsden, V., and D. Wagner, eds. (1995). Literacy among African American youth. Creskill, NJ: Hampton Press.

Jones, Regina, ed. (1996). Handbook of tests and measurements for Black populations. Hampton, VA: Cobbs and Henry.

Kochman, Thomas. (1981). Black and white styles in conflict. NY: Holt Rinehart.

Kochman, Thomas, ed. (1972). Rappin' and stylin' out. Urbana: University of Illinois Press.

Labov, William (1972). Language in the inner city: Studies in the Black English vernacular. Philadelphia: University of Pennsylvania Press.

Lippi-Green, Rosina (forthcoming). English with an accent. London: Routledge.

Mufwene, Salikoko S., John R. Rickford, Guy Bailey and John Baugh, eds. (forthcoming). African American English. London: Routledge.

Rickford, John R., and Lisa Green (forthcoming). African American Vernacular English. Cambridge: Cambridge University Press.

Shuy, Roger W., ed. (1965). Social dialects and language learning. Champaign, IL, National Council of Teachers of English.

Simpkins, G., G. Holt, and C. Simpkins (1977). Bridge: A cross-cultural reading program. Boston: Houghton Mifflin.

Smitherman, Geneva (1986). Talkin and testifyin: The language of Black America. Detroit: Wayne State University Press.

———— (1994). Black Talk. Boston: Houghton Mifflin.

————, ed. (1981). Black English and the Education of Black Children and Youth. Detroit: Center for Black Studies, Wayne State University Press.

Taylor, Hanni U. (1989). Standard English, Black English, and bidialectalism: A controversy. New York: Peter Lang.

Williams, Robert L. (1975). Ebonics: The true language of Black folks. St Louis: Institute of Black Studies.

Wolfram, Walt (1969). A linguistic description of Detroit Negro speech. Washington, D.C.: Center for Applied Linguistics.

———— (1991). Dialects and American English. Englewood Cliffs, NJ: Prentice Hall and Center for Applied Linguistics.

Wolfram, Walter A., and Donna Christian (1989). Dialects and education: Issues and answers. Englewood Cliffs, NJ: Prentice Hall.

Wolfram, Walter A., and Nona Clarke, eds. (1971). Black-White speech relationships. Washington: Center for Applied Linguistics.

JOANNE KILGOUR DOWDY is Associate Professor of Adolescent/Adult Literacy at Kent State University in the Department of Teaching, Leadership, and Curriculum Studies. Her major research is about Black women's experiences with the General Educational Diploma (GED). She has also written a one-woman show, "Between Me and the Lord," which she has performed in the U.S. and Trinidad.

ERNIE SMITH is a Professor of Medicine and Clinical Linguistics in the Department of Internal Medicine, Division of Geriatrics and Gerontology, at Charles R. Drew University of Medicine and Science in Los Angeles. His research is in psycholinguistics and sociolinguistics.

MacArthur fellow LISA DELPIT received the award for Outstanding Contribution to Education in 1993 from the Harvard Graduate School of Education, which hailed her as a "visionary scholar and woman of courage." She is the author of *Other People's Children: Cultural Conflict in the Classroom* (1995, The New Press) and currently holds the Benjamin E. Mays Chair of Urban Educational Leadership at Georgia State University in Atlanta, Georgia.

JUDITH BAKER entered the teaching profession in 1971 and currently teaches English at Madison Park Technical Vocational High School in Boston. Her commitment to equitable education led her to work on teacher-support projects in South Africa and to serve as a teacher consultant with the Boston chapter of the National Writing Project.

MICHAEL STUBBS has been Professor of English Linguistics at the University of Trier, Germany, since 1990. He was previously Professor of English at the Institute of Education, University of London, and Lecturer in Linguistics at the University of Nottingham, UK. He has published widely on educational linguistics, discourse analysis, and corpus linguistics; his most recent book is *Words and Phrases: Corpus Studies of Lexical Semantics* (2001, Blackwell Publishers).

ASA G. HILLARD III is the Fuller E. Callaway Professor of Urban Education at Georgia State University. A teacher, psychologist, and historian, Professor Hilliard's interests include racism and education, public policy, cultural styles, the teaching of African American children, assessment, and child development.

GLORIA J. LADSON-BILLINGS is a professor in the Department of Curriculum and Instruction at the University of Wisconsin, Madison, and a former Senior Fellow in Urban Education at the Annenberg Institute for School Reform at Brown University. Her interests include cultural influences on education and the characteristics of successful teachers of African American children.

VICTORIA PURCELL-GATES is Professor of Literacy at Michigan State University. She is the author of *Other People's Words: The Cycle of Low Literacy* (1995, Harvard University Press). She researches issues of language, literacy, and culture.

HERBERT KOHL has written more than forty books, including the classic *36 Children* (1990, Open University Press). He was founder and first director of Teachers and Writers Collaborative and is currently director of the Center of Teaching Excellence and Social Justice at the University of San Francisco.

GENEVA SMITHERMAN is a Distinguished Professor of English and Director of the African American Language and Literacy Program at Michigan State University. She is currently Chair of the Language Policy Committee's Conference on College Composition and Communication (CCCC) and has received the CCCC 1999 Exemplar Award for her dedication to the English language arts. Smitherman is co-author of 12 books and over 100 articles and papers on language and education, and her current research focuses on language-planning policy in South Africa.

SHUAIB MEACHAM is an Assistant Professor of Literacy Instruction in the School of Education at the University of Delaware. His research applies insights from African American culture and epistemology toward contemporary educational challenges. He is also a "spoken word" poet who works to introduce the form of spoken word poetry into the classroom.

DR. JOAN T. WYNNE is Associate Director of the Alonzo A. Crim Center for Urban Educational Excellence and director of the Urban Teacher Leadership graduate program at Georgia State University. Her current research interests include a study of the consequences of racism on a multi-partner school reform effort underway in a large, southern metropolitan area.